Praise

"I can't tell you how much I admire Kori's bravery. It took great courage to share that pain and it was very moving. This book will be an incredible gift not only for her daughters but for future generations."
SETH DAVIS, ACCLAIMED SPORTS BROADCASTER AND MULTI-PUBLISHED AUTHOR

"Kori is an amazing woman and a great storyteller! She has so much to share, and her story will be so inspirational for others. Very empowering and liberating."
SANDY ABRAMS, ENTREPRENEUR AND PUBLISHED AUTHOR

"Kori is a modern day superhero who embodies true courage, not by defying her insecurities, but by embracing them and turning vulnerability into her own brand of resilience and strength. Her book will help and empower anyone who ever had to face another morning."
BORIS KODJOE, ACTOR

"Kori Clausen is an irreplaceable part of our South Bay community. Her life story is rich and real, and her warmth and kindness have built an extended family that reaches far and anchors deep. *Paddle Out* shares a true story that nobody could dream up, and how it built a family nobody would trade for anything."
AVERY DROST, PRO VOLLEYBALL PLAYER

PADDLE OUT

KORI CLAUSEN
with Jim Martyka

Paddle Out

Published by Hilltop30 Publishing Group, LLC
P.O. Box 93, Bloomington, Indiana 47402
E-mail: tombrew@hilltop30.com
Website: www.hilltop30.com

Cover design: Jessica Dionne, jessicadionne.com
Interior design: Amie McCracken, amiemccracken.com
Cover image: Pressmaster
Editor: Jim Martyka

For Hailey, Leila, Sophia & Sloan

TABLE OF CONTENTS

INTRODUCTION

As I sat on the front stairs of my sister's house in South Carolina, blankly staring into the void and waiting for yet another phone call from the pathologist who was performing the autopsy on my husband's dead body, my anger suddenly rose to pitch level and I had only one thought.

There's no way we're going to have a fucking funeral where we wear all black, and mourn him in a dark and depressing church! Forget his Catholic upbringing, I can't imagine it's what Clint would want. It's not what we want. It's not right. He deserves something more.

The decision was made right there and then to have a paddle out.

Within days, the Manhattan Beach community just south of Los Angeles rallied together to turn this into a truly memorable event worthy of this amazing man who was taken from us way too soon. Friends and neighbors helped spread the word and posters of Clint popped up in storefronts everywhere, including at our restaurant, Clint's dream project that I was now in charge of and completely incapable of running. Everyone loved Clint and they were eager to take part in the celebration.

The paddle out was scheduled for August 22, two weeks after Clint had died. The idea had popped up from a movie we saw about surfing called *Chasing Mavericks*. Also, my daughters had recently returned from a beach camp where they had collected flowers that had washed up on the shore from someone else's own ceremony and it had made an impression. Something like this was beautiful, poignant, and fitting of Clint.

As I lay in bed that morning, balancing a multitude of emotions, fear among them, I realized I would have to speak at this event. I was so sick to my stomach. It would look really bad if I didn't honor him with some great words. Clint was so good at this. He was hilarious and loved talking to people and telling stories... even if they did grow over time! He was calm, sweet, carefree, and always so positive; Clint was just good at everything. I wouldn't be able to do him justice. What's worse is that despite all the time we had together and the love we shared, I seriously couldn't even remember anything besides the way he looked in that hospital bed. The image that was revealed as I opened the white curtain: him lying face up in the hospital bed, he seemed to be staring at the ceiling, there was a white brace of some sort around his neck, and his mouth was open like he was gasping for air. But in actuality it was open because they left the thick white tube in his throat as if they were still working on him. This was what was branded in my mind, and the question to this day is "Why didn't they fix him up for me?" They did nothing.

We all began walking down to the beach; people were coming from everywhere. There were more than three hundred of us, all gathering with surf boards, paddle boards, cameras, and memories. At around 9 a.m., I found myself in the middle of all of them, their sympathetic eyes on me and my four now fatherless daughters, waiting for me to speak. I looked over at Kevin, a man I had met an hour earlier, who gave me a sense of calmness and composedness. He had been recommended by a friend to play some live music as part of the event to help create a sense of serenity. He could see the fear on my face. In his calm voice, he told me, "Just take a deep breath and speak from your heart."

And then I felt something else.

It was a very familiar feeling, the way I used to feel when Clint would wrap me in his arms and hold me. He did it the first night I met him, and it was what made me fall in love with him. That hug. Clint made me feel safe, always. A sense of calmness came over me and then the words just poured out.

"I think it goes without saying how much fun we had with Daddy," I said. "There was never a moment that he was not on. He was always on stage even when he was home—the singing, the dancing, and the joking, was all the time. I was in awe of him. It really wasn't a show how he acted. That's just how he was. He was amazing. "But I just want you to know. Please don't ever think that we don't want to talk about him, because we do. And I never want these girls to forget how wonderful he was...or is and how much he loved them. Thank you so much for coming out. This means a lot, it really does. And he would have loved it. He loved being the center of attention, so it's perfect!"

As everyone laughed, including me for the first time in a couple weeks, I could feel my partner, my rock, smile from above. I handed the mic to my brave daughter Sophia, who read the most beautiful poem, and then my other outgoing daughter Leila who added her own words, joking about him golfing and drinking margaritas somewhere right now. Then our other daughters Hailey and Sloan whispered their own "I love yous."

We all grabbed our boards and headed into the water. As everyone made their way out, I felt embraced by so much love. I was really taking it all in, moment to moment, which flowed together seamlessly. As we paddled out into the Pacific, a circle formed and the five of us were pushed into the center. You could hear a pin drop. It was so calm. No one said anything, and you could just hear the gentle sound of the water. Just as I was wondering what to do next, Clint's best friend said a couple things in honor of Clint. All at once, everyone started smacking the water, whistling and cheering. The look of the splashing water created a kind of barrier to close us all in the circle. I like to think it sealed us all together for that one moment, and I will always remember how safe I felt, like I wasn't alone. It was the most amazing moment, and I felt so happy that we made this happen for him. I didn't want it to end. As we were cheering, the group went from a huge circle of a couple hundred people to a huge huddle as everyone closed in on us, throwing flowers and showing their love.

There was a drone there shooting footage of the paddle out that day. When we watched what it had recorded later, we were blown away to see that the group of paddlers, these people who loved Clint and supported us, had coincidentally (or maybe not?) formed the shape of a heart around us. That picture, captured from

the drone, is framed and hangs in the living room of the home we built together, the home that still feels a little emptier, but overflowing with love...

I struggled coming up with a title for this book, but when *Paddle Out* was suggested, it just made sense. Not only did it take me back to that amazing day when we were all able to pay tribute to a great man, but it also implies a journey, living in the moment, and the drive to take a risk and do something grand. We all have those moments where we have to paddle out, to leave the safety of the shore, to face our fears and see where the water takes us.

That's what this book is for me.

As I'm embarking on this journey, I don't really know what's going to come of this. I don't even really know why I started writing in the first place, other than that I was guided. But as I did, I realized this project was a tribute to an incredible man, a legacy for four amazing young girls, and catharsis for me. I have experienced a lot in my life, including a lot of tragedy before that fateful night. That's led to a constant struggle in many ways, one that I continue to fight. It hasn't been a pretty or an easy life, by any means.

But the fight is absolutely worth it.

I've learned a lot, or rather, I'm *learning* a lot. I hope that by sharing some of what I've learned, it helps anyone reading this. I don't intend this to be a self-help book. I don't want to tell anyone what to think or do. I just want to show how facing these things, and building toward acceptance, is how I've learned to get out of my own way and live the life I deserve. And if that helps give perspective to someone reading this, that's wonderful.

I can begin with the simple fact that life is difficult. Period. This is a never-ending process. Accepting that actually makes it a little easier and acceptance is something I'm working on. So is making the right choices, the ones that are better for my life and my well-being. Life is meant to be lived at its fullest, no matter the circumstances or the challenges that pop up along the way.

It has taken me a long time, but I have learned that I am worthy of happiness. I am worthy of a good life. Clint helped teach me that. My daughters constantly remind me. I'm still working on believing it fully. I am trying to accept my past, live in the present and look to a brighter future. I'm hoping by sharing my story and inviting you along as I go through this process, it will help you do the same.

So hop on that board and come with me. The ocean is large and deep and there are many, many waves. But there is also a beauty in paddling out, and beyond the waves, there is calm and peace. We're all here together, and we're forming a giant heart.

CHAPTER 1
I CAN REMEMBER
THE LOVE

It's a weird feeling when you look back at the absolute worst day of your life and wish you could go back there. I think of that day and I can't help it. My heart yearns to return, even knowing what was going to happen that night and in the days, months, and years to follow. I think it's because now, after a few years have passed (and countless therapy sessions), I can remember all the joy we experienced as a family that day. I can remember how important and special it was that we were all together on the tail end of an extended family vacation. I can remember the jokes, the smiles, the laughter. I can remember the love.

I can also remember that day as the last one in a very long time where I wasn't feeling that old familiar struggle, the one that threatened to destroy all I had built.

All *we* had built.

Love is the only thing that has gotten me through the last few years. Sure I've had a deep-rooted and well-tested survival instinct, responsibilities as a mother, and an against-all-odds passion for life that has kept me moving, hanging on desperately to the person I am and the person I want to be. But ultimately, it's this love that we experienced on that fateful night, together as a family, that has guided me along through the good times and the bad.

It's a love that I learned from my husband Clint, who died on August 8, 2014.

The week before he died was one I had been excited about for quite a while...and it was everything I had hoped it would be. I could not have asked for a more amazing trip. When our family of six—me, Clint, and our four beautiful daughters—left for South Carolina, we had no idea that we would return home a family of five. In a small way, I'm almost glad Clint's passing happened on the last night so we could at least have that amazing vacation to remember and cherish once the pain associated with it dissipated.

At my mother's urging, we had gone out there, along with my brother Jason's family, my sister Kelly and her family, my Aunt Marianne, and my stepbrother Mike for a big vacation, the first time my entire side of the family had been together in six years. That meant nine kids in total, some of them meeting for the first time, though you would have never known by the way they all played together. It was a beautiful trip, a wonderful gift from my mother, who rented the house for us. It was a chance for us all to connect together as a family and I think, looking back, it was a way to make sure we would all be there for each other when disaster struck.

On that final day, we had plans to have a photographer come to take pictures of the entire extended family. We were all supposed to wear jeans and white shirts to match. After a day in the sun and water, everyone was frantic and running late, trying to get ready. Or rather, we were trying to get *them* ready. The kids were whining about changing, not wanting to get out of their bathing suits that they had spent the entire vacation in. As the photographer arrived, I pulled my sister aside.

"This is silly," I said. "Let all the kids wear their suits. They look adorable and it's more natural."

Of course, the adults were all changed out of their suits and looking good...except for Clint who had an odd shirt and shorts combination. Clint was a lot of things: sweet, calm, patient, easy-going, loving, and always ready to laugh or get those around him to laugh. But he didn't always have the best eye for fashion.

I giggled and said, "Clint, that doesn't make sense. You have a pair of shorts that match perfectly sitting right there on the bed."

"Would you like me to change it?" he asked in one of his signature silly voices. I loved how that man was always in a playful mood.

"Well, why not at least match for the family photos that we'll have forever," I replied with a smile, a smile that he told me time and time again he loved.

We both laughed, and I left the room. It seemed to take forever for him to change his shorts so I went to check on him. He didn't see me at first, and I got the strangest feeling as I watched him slowly put his belt through the loop holes on his shorts. I thought to myself, "Why is he moving so slow? It's so weird."

That was the first sign. And I missed it. Rather, I didn't think anything too seriously of it. Then again, who would? There have been times over the past few years that I have blamed myself for not noticing something was wrong that day. I've wondered if I had said or done something, if we could have saved him. Everyone who experiences a sudden loss like this wonders the same thing. It's inevitable. It's also nothing but self-destructive to blame yourself. Clint was in good shape and good health. There were no prior warning signs. The things that I noticed that day were small oddities that were quickly forgotten in the joy we were sharing together. The photographers arrived, and we all had so much fun taking the pictures, pictures that I still look at all the time as the final moments we were a full, happy family. They followed us down to the beach and back to the balcony of the house, taking several

posed and candid pictures of the kids playing and goofing around. Then we decided to take separate family photos. When it was our turn, we all just piled on and around Clint, just like we always did. I jumped on his back and the girls were all standing on the balcony railing leaning on him.

Clint was six-foot-three and a big strong guy. He liked to jokingly compare himself to Arnold Schwarzenegger. But he was now having trouble holding me, and once again, another odd feeling passed through me. He was breathing heavier and looked red and sweaty. He was clearly struggling, even as he continued to smile and joke around. Maybe it was the humidity, I thought. Once again, the moment and the worry passed as we hopped off him and played around for the next picture.

After the photographers left, Clint went with my brother-in-law Matt into town to pick up some pizzas. It seemed to take forever and when they got back, we learned that Clint had made them make a special trip to get me sushi. I love sushi, always have. Now I would have been quite content with pizza, but Clint apparently insisted on going to get me sushi...which was unusual as well. Clint wasn't the kind of person to give small gifts or go out of his way to do little things like that. Oh, he showed me in plenty of other ways how much he loved me, but sweet little gestures weren't really his thing. This is something I would think about later as well.

Normally on a Friday evening around 6:30 p.m., we would have been at our home for movie night. All of the girls--and I do mean all of us--would have been cuddled around Clint. He was so warm and cozy. In his arms was always the favorite spot. Even as babies, the girls all seemed to fall asleep once they were with him. I know it was my favorite place. It was that all-encompassing embrace, the same one he gave me that first day we met. I don't take naps and even I would feel my eyelids get heavy when I was cuddled next to him.

As that evening settled in, Jason, Kelly, Clint, and I were in the living room in the big house we were staying in on Isle of Palms. We were thinking back on the week and what a great trip it had been, chatting about everything we had done, how the cousins had all connected and laughing at our experiences. Laughter was something that always happened when Clint was around. In fact, the night before, we were essentially in the same place and Clint had been sharing some of his silly stories of the restaurant we owned, to the delight of my family. I had worked there for a time, but found it wasn't for me. That night he jokingly said he wanted me to come back, and I quickly held my hands out in front of me and said, "I want nothing to do with it." Less than twenty-four hours later, I would be the owner and president.

I remember at one point, looking over at him and smiling. I also took just a half second to check on him.

Fifteen minutes earlier, I was upstairs in our room packing up our things. He came in the room with a puzzled look on his face. He told me he had a headache. He then walked over to the dresser and grabbed a little bottle of aspirin. He sat on the bed, took one out, and quickly swallowed it. I asked him why he thought had a headache. He looked me straight in the eyes took a deep breath and said, "I don't know?"

What was odd was that there was something questioning in his voice, something he really didn't understand. He had a very peculiar look on his face, almost like there was something else he was feeling. Without saying anything else, he then turned around and left the room and I continued packing.

I busily scurried from room to room picking up things that were scattered here and there. As I passed by the room where they were all sitting, he invited me to come sit on his lap. I hesitated because I am a freak, and the thought of not having everything perfectly packed and ready to go made me very uneasy. But then he asked again in a very loving voice. There was an extra tenderness about it and it stopped me.

"Mommy, come sit on my lap for a minute." He called me Mommy and I called him Daddy ever since the girls were born. That's just something that two people who were in love and raised beautiful children together did. Or maybe they didn't. We didn't care. It's what we did, and it was one of a million ways we showed our love for each other.

Against my natural instincts to finish my task, something told me to listen. Thank God I did. I stopped what I was doing and went to join him. My sister, who was just as crazy as me, stopped what she was doing and came to join us as well. I stretched out across Clint's lap, enveloping myself in his arms one last time. As if controlled by something bigger than us, we were led to each other, to be with each other, heart-to-heart and connected at the end.

While I was sitting on his lap, he asked me if I was comfortable. He was holding me like a parent would hold their child. I was lying across his lap, my head resting on his arm. I told him I was, and a quick thought went through my mind about how sweet it was for him to ask. The very next moment, I felt him take a large inhale, his entire chest completely expanded. Then all I heard was a loud exhale, and suddenly...

The arm that was holding me dropped to the side. When it fell, so did everything else. It would be a long time before I would be able to pick up all the pieces.

I still am.

CHAPTER 2
HOW DID I
GET HERE?

How did I get here?

This is a question I ask myself all the time. It's one I've been asking since I first started writing this book a few years ago. How did I become a mother of four beautiful daughters, a restaurant owner against my will, and a widow at the young age of forty-three?

Seriously.

How did I go from a simple Midwestern girl with high hopes and a yearning for love, an ambitious and successful dancing career, and a lot of obstacles (many self-imposed) to a beach mom with a big heart who is working, struggling, and fighting to be the best she can be for herself and her daughters?

I hate using words like strange, bizarre, or weird because I believe that one day all of this will make complete sense. It is, in my opinion, part of a plan. There is a Divine Order, where everything that is happening can really be traced back to an origin and from that origin comes our purpose. In a sense, that's part of why I'm writing this book; to trace back to that origin, figure out the path, and see what I can find about my purpose, or at least some kind of explanation for it all.

I've always believed our loved ones who have passed on are lovingly smiling down on us because they now know the truth. That brings me comfort. They get the chance to see it and watch as it plays out in the lives of those they've loved. I've asked mine for a hint, just a peek at that plan from time to time, but I'm mostly met with silence.

Mostly.

I know Clint is looking down and, in his own way, enjoying watching me ponder this Divine Order in a seemingly chaotic world. I can envision the big grin on my husband's face because he knows something before I do, and because he knows eventually I'll see it as well. Honestly, I feel like I'm on that path as I'm learning to surrender more. I am fascinated by the idea that everything is made of energy and it's this energy that connects all of us on a universal level, that I am the sum of all the things that have brought me to this point right here, right now. I've spent most of my life forcing things, instead of stepping back and actually surrendering. I have realized what is meant to be will be, and that it all comes from a truth I feel and perhaps generate, deep in my core. I'm trying to tap into that energy, discover that origin, and understand my path. Looking back over the course of my life, with the guidance of what I learned from an incredible friend, lover, husband, and father, is helping me do so.

I remember when I was child, I was asked the question, "If you could look into a glass ball and see your future, would you?" There was no hesitation in my answer. "Of course I would!" I mean, how awesome to be able to see your whole life played out right before your eyes!

Ask me that question today and my answer would be the polar opposite. If someone would have said, "So here is the deal. You are one of the lucky few who will get the man of your dreams. He is hysterical, smart, athletic, and very good looking. He is going to love you more then you will ever realize...but there is a catch. He is going to die of a massive heart attack fourteen years into your marriage and you will be left to raise your four daughters on your own."

What would I have done? I honestly don't know. Here we are, totally in love and building a life together and that bomb gets dropped. I realize with a terminal illness this is how people have to live day to day. The upside would be that maybe we would have lived differently, knowing we were on borrowed time. We also would have been able to say all the things we wanted to say, even (or especially) goodbye. Right after his passing, I lived with guilt and regret for not saying or doing more to show him I loved him. I know my oldest daughter Hailey lived with guilt as well. On the day he died, he had asked her to lunch, and being a normal child, she wanted to play with her cousins instead, so she didn't go. She really struggled with that. We all struggled.

Still, I don't think I would have wanted to know. I wouldn't have wanted to sacrifice the love, dreams, and hope we had in the process, living moment to moment with this amazing man. Believe it or not, the only way for me to look at this whole situation is to be thankful. The truth is I have made a lot of bad choices in my life. Trying to understand why is part of what the process of writing this book is all about. It's also because I'm afraid of making those choices again.

I have already made a few.

He was a blessing, and one that I believed I *willed* into my life. That's right; it was the inner child, that little girl in me. It was what *she* wanted, what she yearned for deep in her core, with all her insecurities and fears and the trauma she experienced, especially when it came to the men she loved. I was always day-dreaming, imagining, making things up in my mind to bring me comfort and make me feel good. I believe the more I did of this, eventually the universe gave back. I just had to be present and aware enough to see it and fully understand. When I look back on what I would dream about when it came to a man that could love me, I realize it was Clint. He was in my day dreams, the prince in my fairy tale as a young girl. He was what I wanted deep in my soul, even at all the times I thought I was undeserving of it. Our mind has the power to build a wall but our heart knows better. I was sending out energy my whole life, even as I went time and time again down the wrong path. Eventually the universe responded and rewarded. It can't be avoided. The heart always wins.

Now, years after he passed, I'm still left wondering and exploring if the universe brought him to me as a reward for listening to my heart, a relief from all the previous struggles, for a fleeting period of happiness and bliss, or for something more. I wonder now if he was brought to teach me something and to keep teaching me even after he was gone.

I didn't expect to write this book. I do not write. I have never even remotely felt the need to write, nor have I ever had the confidence in thinking that I could. That being said, in the past few years, the idea of writing has come up numerous times. It is kind of like that annoying sound of your fire alarm when the batteries die. It does not stop until you are forced to climb on the ladder and change the batteries. I also have these spiritual cards that I turn to when I'm questioning and stressed about things. There is one that kept turning up time and time again. It had the ascended master "Thoth" (pronounced tay-ho-tay) on it. The heading on the top of the card read "Write."

I've heard that writing can be very healing. Getting things out and down on paper is a kind of therapy. I have also heard some people say that when they began to write they were so inspired that the words just wrote themselves. This annoyed me beyond belief. I mean, come on, the words wrote themselves? That is ridiculous!

And yet, here I am, writing and being guided by forces greater than me. I'm surrendering to this process because once again, there must be a purpose...and I think this time I might understand it.

Writing this book is me paddling out farther than I ever have before, and I have to admit, I'm just as afraid as I am excited and inspired. I have a story that needs to be told, not just to pay homage to a man who deserves a monument, and to help preserve a legacy for my daughters, but also maybe to speak toothers that have experienced great loss and tragedy and might bedrifting, lost and unsure of how to swim back to land.

But even more than that, I need to do it for me. I have some things I have hidden for way too long...even from Clint. Though losing my husband was the greatest loss of my life, it wasn't my only one. In fact, as I look back and uncover all that I had buried for so long, I realize I have almost lost myself many times over the years.

Even now I'm still fighting to survive. And my god, it's so much harder to do without him here.

I am a human, in this physical body, trying to navigate my life to the best of my abilities. I am a wife and a mother who never realized the strength I held within until faced with the death of my husband, my lover, my best friend. The challenge is to find happiness no matter what curveballs this life throws at us. We are meant to be happy and we are capable beyond belief, but we get lost along the way.

I sometimes feel like I'm still lost.

It's not as bad as it was right after Clint passed. I am getting better. But there are demons that I have to deal with on a daily basis, familiar demons that have been around since long before I met Clint. I have to be strong, not just for my girls, but also for me. I grew up with loss, as well as a series of, for a lack of a better way of saying it, *bad* decisions that culminated in horrible situations that could have, and perhaps should have ended my life well before Clint came along. I know I'm capable of making them again and that's terrifying. Over the course of my life, I have dealt with abuse, addiction, a lifelong eating disorder, a suicide attempt, a low sense of self-worth and the guilt of repressing much of this and not sharing it with someone who I know would have loved me regardless. I'm not writing about this to be a victim. I hate the idea of being a victim. I'm owning my past. Rather, I feel like I owe it to Clint, my daughters, and anyone reading this book to finally unload everything, to show that no matter what you experience (and what you hide), you can always overcome it...and be honest in sharing it.

I'm also writing because as I mentioned, I'm still fighting. When I met Clint, the addictions and disorders, the darkness in my life, went away...in a sense. I actually buried it, which I knew wasn't healthy, but I was distracted enough by building a beautiful life with this man and our four daughters, that I was happy enough to keep it at bay. When Clint passed, the darkness came back with a vengeance. I began to slip right back into some of the old bad habits and almost lost myself again.

I am just now in the process of coming back. Writing this book is part of my fight for survival. I am surrendering to that process, embracing it and all that it brings. I have lived by fear and ego for a good part of my life, but no more. In the end, truth always wins and I will be truthful in this process, no matter what that means.

So much time in my life has been spent keeping others and their feelings at the front of my mind. I always want to make sure everyone else is taken care of first. But now it's time to focus on myself, not just for me, but for my daughters and everyone else who loves me.

My daughters, I can't say enough about them. While all four of them are unique, they work together as a beautiful, loving, and caring unit, and one that has always been supportive of me, no matter what. I'm fighting for them, to be the best mom I can be now and forever.

For Clint. God bless that man, he was my security and my confidence. He was my strength. I'm trying to get back to where I was when I felt his arms around me. And being honest is doing that. I believe that the truth will set you free. I cannot express enough the sense of lightness I have felt by letting go, and how this has propelled me forward. It has given me new life.

Like any memoir, especially from someone who has dealt with tragedy, this book is part catharsis for me. It's also a confession. It's also a story of love and overcoming struggle. It highlights the wonderful benefits of that surrendering to the process, letting go of the fear and laughing at the pain. At its heart, it's a story about finding and creating happiness and believing in something more.

Of course, it's also a tribute to Clint. In fact, this is just as much his book as it is mine. It's been surprising that these words, even about the harder times, are coming easier than I ever would have expected. Clint is that force guiding me. He is helping me tell this story and it feels so good to have him helping me on this journey.

I often separate my life into two categories: BC and AD, or "Before Clint" and "After Died." But honestly, I think it might be what happened in the middle, the years I had with Clint, and how we grew, learned, and loved together, that might provide me with the answers I'm looking for in my life. Both in examining my past, and continuing the fight and building a better future for me and my daughters.

I can't quite put into words all the emotions I'm feeling as I start this story (see, I told you I wasn't a writer!). It's hard to look back over your life and share it openly and honestly...the good, the bad, and the ugly. But I know it's what I must do. I'm at a crossroads and there are so many paths I can take, some of them quite dangerous. I want to make sure I'm venturing forth down the best one, the one worthy of Clint and my daughters. The one worthy of myself.

Sometimes, before we move forward, we need to look back. That helps us stay in touch with that Divine Order, to make sure we're truly fulfilling our destiny.

CHAPTER 3
THE LOSS OF
STABILITY

We all experience loss and those losses are arguably our most crucial and influential moments in terms of how they shape our personalities, our paths, or at the very least, our outlook on our existence. Loss comes in all shapes and sizes, and amazingly almost always at critical times in our personal growth. If you think back to the key moments in your life, you'll identify several that are associated with a loss of some kind, good or bad.

How we handle that loss--the emotions we feel, the choices we make, where those moments lead us--are key factors in defining our lives.

I have experienced a lot of loss in my life, starting at an early age. Although difficult, I believe it has made me stronger. Overall (and especially on the surface), I have had a very good life. But there have been a good number of obstacles along the way, things that have led me down that dark and dangerous path. To understand where those obstacles came from, how that path manifested itself, so I can avoid it, I need to explore those moments of loss and what they meant for my life.

So in order for things to make some sense now, I have to go back to the very beginning, to BC...

On July 20, 1970, in the Midwestern town of Toledo, Ohio, I was born to Margretta Renz Fleck and Ronald James Keefer at Flower Hospital. My parents didn't know what they were having until I was born so I was named "Kori," which (luckily) meant "Little Girl" in Greek. Although I myself do not remember this event, my mother can account for every moment and has often shared with me what life was like when I came into the world.

I had the biggest, darkest brown eyes, eyes my mother said could melt anyone's heart. I could never hide a surprised reaction because they would get even bigger upon noticing or hearing something. I remember my great grandmother used to say to me, whenever I would cry, that "brown eyes should never be blue." I loved her sweet voice when she would say this, but I didn't really understand it. Personally I always wished my eyes *were* blue.

I was very quiet and very shy as a small child, not at all like I am today. My mom and older sister said I was reserved, someone who just appeared to be taking everything in. I was apparently a very good girl who didn't cause many problems, and I seemed to like everyone. However, by all accounts, I was also extremely sensitive and vulnerable; my feelings could get hurt easily. When I was five, my sister and I were flower girls in my aunt's wedding. We were at the rehearsal and the priest asked me to hand over the rings. Although he was joking, and everyone around me laughed, I was hurt. I ran to another area of the church and couldn't stop crying. He scared me, and I didn't like the way he turned the attention onto me. The way someone would look at me would go straight to my core. I would always feel as if I had done something wrong, even when I hadn't. I would describe this feeling like those dogs that always walk around with their tail between their legs.

That hasn't changed much.

My first few years in this world were filled with relative happiness, the innocence of youth, and a contentment of being part of a family. We lived in a simple and sweet red house at the end of a cul-de-sac, my parents and I, along with my older sister Kelly (who was four years older) and my baby brother Jason (who was four  years younger). We would go to the country club at times and even trips to the lake as a family. All seemed well...on the surface.

But there was fighting between my parents. A lot of fighting. And that fighting made a deep and lasting impression on me, even at a young age. My older sister Kelly remembers more of it than I do, and she described the fighting as demeaning, two people with triggers that could be immature in how they handled each other. My father had a temper, and I know he liked taking it out on things, sometimes physically, including my mother. If you grow up with it, you begin to think that's the norm, but I would remember going to our neighbors' houses or visiting childhood friends and getting a different "family" feel at those places. And for some reason, not having that same kind of family feeling made me feel not good enough or less than. Our family unit quickly began to degrade even more as my parents fought more and more often, until finally I experienced the first real significant loss of my life.

The loss of stability.

The day our parents told us they were getting divorced, I

remember, was a sunny day. My parents were sitting on some sort of chair together. Actually, it was a love seat, which is rather ironic. We were in the living room, or was it the family room? I don't know, and I never could figure out the difference between the two. Do you live in the family room or hang out with your family in the living room? I digress...

Kelly and I were sitting criss-cross applesauce on the floor looking up at them. Their mouths were moving, so I knew they were talking. I just wasn't sure what they were saying. All of a sudden, I looked at my sister and noticed she was crying, so I figured I should probably cry too, and I did. Kelly was always the one who made me feel safe and comfortable, so I relied on her. When I saw she was upset, I knew something was wrong. The fact that they were sitting together should have been a dead give-away.

My sister Kelly remembers that day as the moment her childhood ended. It was the end of the idea of family, her emotional security, and a whole lot more. Kelly said at that point she started to notice the ugliness the world held. I think I experienced those things as well, but I simply couldn't define them. I just stared back and forth from my parents to Kelly with my big brown eyes full of tears wondering what all this meant. It wouldn't be until much later when I would understand how much everything really changed that day.

During the divorce, Kelly, Jason, and I were split up...and so began a rather chaotic and confusing time of shuffling us kids from place to place and life-shaping experience to life-shaping experience as we all tried desperately to grab a foothold on our lives.

For a brief time, I actually stayed with a friend's family. They already had four children—twin girls who were older than me and twin boys who were about my same age. They had a huge, white, colonial house with a wraparound porch, a ton of land, a pool, and a scary barn. Even as a young child, this house seemed far from civilization. I remember the long drive, my head lying on my mother's lap. When we arrived, I still wasn't sure why I was there, but they showed me a room that they had made up just for me. That was the moment I realized I was staying and I got a sinking feeling in my gut. Shortly after, watching my mother drive away brought such pain to my heart. Not wanting to disappoint anyone, I appeared fine on the surface, but I was completely deflated. I can only imagine how she felt. Though I was only there for the summer, it felt like a lifetime. It was my first real experience with abandonment...and those first experiences stay with you.

At four years old, I felt broken, lost, and so confused inside. That might seem like a lot for a four-year-old to experience, but I was in touch with my emotions at a young age and I knew what pain was.

Kelly wanted to live with my dad, and despite my mother's protests, she went with him. Not long after, when my mom realized she couldn't support us on her wages—and with my father refusing to pay court-ordered child support—I was given over to him as well. Jason soon followed. It was such a strange feeling being passed around. There was never a strong foundation upon which to build my sense of self-worth. I was not comfortable around my father; it felt like something was missing, mainly love. As a child I was always on my best behavior to see how to get that love from him. It never seemed to work. I was confused and it took a long time to realize that I didn't have to be a certain way. Love should just *be* there and if it isn't, I cannot make someone love me. It was this next year of living with my father that formed my first impressions of men, especially when it came to fear, a loss of protection, and feelings of unworthiness. I would come to feel like I was simply a burden, nothing more.

We moved a lot in that time, but each place had a significant memory. There was an apartment in Toledo. We slept in sleeping bags in the dining room where otherwise there would have been a dinner table. We each had a cardboard box for storing our clothes. Each night, we would roll out our sleeping bags, and then roll them back up upon waking the next morning. Looking back on it, that situation was not ideal, but for me, it felt like a constant sleepover. It wasn't the worst thing, especially because I was with my sister. My father, on the other hand, was starting to reveal his true nature. Or perhaps, I was just starting to mature enough to see him for who and what he really was. It wasn't pretty. Things got to be a little confusing when we were with my father. He had two girlfriends at the same time. There was Linda, who was so nice. She had blonde hair, a beautiful smile, and was very friendly and sweet to us. The other one was Kathy, who had dark hair, was very high maintenance, and wasn't as sweet. My sister and I would have no problem distinguishing between the two of them; we knew who we liked to be around. Unfortunately, keeping their names straight was an issue. Kathy couldn't understand why we called her Linda all the time, and Linda couldn't understand why we called her Kathy. There was only one person they could talk to about that, and he wasn't very happy with us! The last time I remember seeing Linda, Kelly and I were sitting in my father's car. She and my father were standing outside next to the car, and they were arguing loudly. Linda was yelling and crying, and she threw a glass, shattering it on the ground. She eventually left, and my father got in the car. He looked straight ahead, and the energy radiating off of him concerned both me and Kelly. We sat in complete silence as we drove away.

So that left Kathy.

My father was selfish and inconsiderate, especially when it came to our relationship with our mother. The way he spoke about my mother was so wrong and hurtful. Looking back, I fully realize now that "family" was never a concept that was important to my father, which made it even more difficult for children who were trying to find something to grasp onto.

There also was an old cottage on Clark Lake in Ann Arbor, Michigan that we lived in for a while. The guy who owned it was a friend of my dad's named Renny, but I never met him. One Easter

Sunday, Kelly and I were so excited to learn that my mother and old neighbor were driving from Toledo to come see us for the day. So my father and Kathy thought this would be the perfect time to enjoy the day out with the kids. We ended up at a bar where endless drinking and games of pool were going on. I recall thinking the entire time that we should probably head back to Renny's house to see Mom. I was very confused because Kathy and my father knew she was coming. At one point I was in the bathroom crying, and Kathy was consoling me. I just couldn't understand why we weren't leaving. When we finally did arrive back home, it was pretty late. I noticed as we pulled up the driveway that the only thing waiting for us were gifts on the doorstep. I don't remember what was left for Kelly or Jason, but for me there was a ceramic piggy bank. It was white and had a green ceramic bow tied around its big belly. I loved it! My great grandmother had made our favorite coffee toffee pie, which was left there as well. As much as I enjoyed the gifts, I also know I had a big ball of pain welled up inside my heart. I had just wanted to see my mommy, and I knew that my father had taken that from me.

Jason, though still a baby, often received the worst of it. Kathy would take her frustrations out on him. He went to the bathroom in the tub once, and my sister and I had to sit outside of the bathroom while we listened to Kathy spank him over and over. He was crying so hard that our hearts were broken. She would also leave him in what we called the "the scary room." It was an upstairs room in the back that faced the lake. It was a room that would normally be open for the summer months but closed off for the winter months. He would be in his crib just crying and crying.

I remember another time Kathy threw him and he landed on his bottom and slid across the floor. His head fell back and hit the ground hard. This was the time Kelly finally had enough and told my mom. I remember standing in a dark hallway, excited because my mom was now coming to "visit." I overheard Kathy talking to my dad in a very irritated voice about my mother. "She is being so nice to him!" I immediately got that sick feeling in my gut. Kathy and Dad got in a fight, and Dad was so mad because Mom had been told about what Kathy did. I remember Kelly and I both sitting in his front car seat, and we were so quiet. We were so scared. He got in the car, took his clipboard, and threw it, hitting me. I just remember this feeling of sadness. This insecure feeling became the norm.

He could also be malicious. One year, my father gave Kelly and me his melted down wedding ring. I didn't understand what this was at the time; I just remember wishing it was in the shape of a teddy bear or something fun like a charm. Instead it was a flat blob hanging on a gold chain. Looking back, I'm sure this was a way for my father to rub it in my mother's face. He knew something like this would hurt, and he did it anyway, not realizing or caring what it would do to us.

Between moments like this and my father's temper, I developed distrust and a sense of fear around men that would follow me through my adolescence. I was always hesitant around my friends' fathers, always scared they were going to get mad at something or other. Then I would get to know them and begin to realize that not all fathers were like mine.

I remember so much yelling at nothing but his own frustra-tions in life. My sister remembers that at one time early on, he was a gifted salesman with a big ego, but it didn't last. He spent most of his life playing catch up, ignoring and avoiding financial responsibilities, and trying to be the big man he thought he was. He wasn't. Ever. At least not to us.

I remember a time he was supposed to pick me up from school and never did. I waited until just before dark. Every car that pulled around the corner, I just knew was his. This was how I spent the next twenty years, always giving him chances to come around. Every time, he would disappoint. After having my own children, I don't understand the disconnect that he had with us as our father. My sister and brother wrote him off years ago, but for some reason I thought maybe things would change. Despite my anger with him, I found myself always hoping for his love, guidance, and acceptance. I kept waiting for him to be a father.

I absorbed all of this. I personally think we do absorb all of these experiences, not just in our conscious and subconscious, but even deeper, on a cellular level. They make up who and what we become. My time with him was short but impactful.

There was one moment where I truly felt what might have been his love. I was six years old and leaving to go back to Toledo after a visit with him in his trailer park in Michigan. He was saying goodbye, and I was actually crying because I had to go back to my mother in Ohio. I cannot remember if I was sad to leave my sister or if it was because of leaving him. He was holding a bowl of ice cream and feeding me a spoonful. He had gotten down on one knee and was consoling me. Something about that made me feel loved.

But even that was confusing, and I couldn't tell if it was maybe relief on his end or pity on mine. I just don't know, and that's all I've got. From a father, that's not enough. No matter how many times over the years I would reach out to him, he always seemed to act so sincere but he never would follow through with the sincerity. I always felt bad for him even though he didn't deserve it. I have been that way my whole life with men, really.

Which, as you'll soon see, has led to some major problems.

During these early years of my life, I also started to get these terrible headaches. I must have been around six years old when they started. They were so powerful. All of the pain I felt would crumple up into a huge ball and nestle in behind my right eye. That pain was excruciating. My vision blurred and all I would want to do was cry, but even that would be too painful. I lay in a dark room, and literally hummed to myself. The pain would get so bad that eventually I would vomit, and then just like that, it was gone.

My mother took me to a couple doctors who ran several tests on my brain, but there was nothing conclusive to explain the headaches. My mother's personal thoughts were that I was keeping a lot of emotions inside and was unable to articulate what was going on. It was soon decided that I should see a therapist. I do not remember these actual sessions with him or what was discussed, but I will never forget this round room with carpeted walls and a lot of pillows. My favorite part was going in and throwing pillows around and laughing. It was these moments where I felt a fleeting sense of childhood bliss.

The therapist agreed with my mother. The headaches were being brought on by stress and a bottling up of emotions that honestly plagues me to this day.

Kelly, for some reason, had decided to stay with my father even after Jason and I left. Her life, for the next several years, essentially consisted of being a live-in maid and nanny, cleaning the house for our father and Kathy, as well as helping to raise their son Andrew. She did nothing else. I missed her terribly. In the years that I was separated from her, we had a special song between the two of us, a song most people would have had with their boyfriend or girl-friend. It was "Love on the Rocks" by Neil Diamond. Yes, strange choice, but keep in mind we were kids and didn't really under-stand the lyrics or message. To this day, when that song plays (which is hardly ever) it still brings tears to my eyes.

On the rare occasion when I would visit, I would have to help Kelly do dishes from these overly extravagant meals that Kathy made, using all the dishes. Our doing dishes and singing together were the only good memories. We didn't play, we never felt comfortable just playing, so we would clean. I remember it felt like there was this underlying guilt, that this is what we should be doing. My sister said it was never asked but just assumed because that was the role she had moved into and that's how she received love, recognition, and acceptance. She couldn't put this into words as a child, but it was how she felt *comfortable*. So when Jason and I would come to visit, I would follow her lead. She would be excited for weeks, knowing we were coming to visit. She loved us all being together. Plus the atmosphere would change drastically because Kathy would be on her best behavior...generally.

As much as I loved seeing her, I hated it there. One evening I was missing my mom so bad, but I didn't want them to know. I did everything from pinching myself, holding my breath, and biting my lip to not cry. All of a sudden I lost it, just like that, standing in the middle of the room. I began sobbing, it was loud. But they let me call Mom, and I instantly felt better.

Stress is the only thing that makes sense.

Stress is my father's legacy. Anger, pain, fear, a misplaced sense of self, and no real sense or understanding of stability. That's what I got out of my first real loss and those aftereffects would shape a majority of my decisions over the rest of my life, up to and including today. Yes, the losses we experience in those early years never leave us.

In many ways, they *are* us.

CHAPTER 4
A STORM WAS COMING

While I was still living with my father, we spent some time in "The Landings," which was a really nice trailer park that my dad was managing in Michigan. My dad would get so upset when we called it that. In fact, my brother Jason used to call it a "camper park" and my dad would yell, "It's a mobile home park!"

Whatever it was, it was settled on Devil's Lake. In my short time there, it earned its name.

On a rather cloudy day, ominous-looking, my dad's friend Jay stopped by with his two sons and Amy, who was his girlfriend's daughter. Amy was someone I would play with growing up. She was cute and shy like me, and to this day, when I think of her I envision Shirley Temple. Maybe it was because she looked like her. I really don't remember, I just remember I felt good when I was around her. While I waved hello to Amy on that fateful day, I didn't realize I was waving goodbye at the same time. The clouds got darker as Jay spoke with my dad, letting him know he was taking the kids out on the lake in their boat before the weather got bad. A storm was coming.

And the lake was very choppy.

I had a bad feeling. I know this for sure, though it wasn't that abnormal back when I was a child. As previously mentioned, I was not settled in my life and I often was filled with anxiety and fear. But this was different. I looked up at those clouds, and the day just seemed sad.

Later that afternoon, there was quite a commotion going on outside. Everyone was panicking, and I was trying to figure out what the noise was all about. I would learn later that Amy had drowned. Apparently, when they took the boat out on the rough waters, nobody was wearing life jackets. Jay was driving, and one of the boys got his attention, telling him that Amy had fallen out of the boat. Jay dove in without stopping. The boys barely knew how to drive the boat. They tried to circle around but couldn't get close to where they were. Jay was able to find her and for a brief moment or two, he got her in his arms. But she slipped out, and the waves prevented him from seeing her under the water, and he lost her.

I don't think I understood what was happening, only that something was very wrong. The next day, a bunch of people went out on the lake to drag for her body. It was very calm, and the lake was smooth like ice. I sat on the edge of the boat with my arm hanging over the side looking closely in the water. I know she had a blue suit on, so I stared hard into the water. I wanted to be the one to find her. They ended up closing the lake down, and she was found by a fisherman a few days later.

This was my first experience with death, with a very particular and final kind of loss. It was sudden, tragic, heart-breaking, and difficult to understand. It was final.

It also wouldn't be my last experience of this kind, not by a long shot. Death has played a factor in my life long before what happened with my husband. With each death came a major shift in my life. I would come face to face with it often, especially in my childhood. In fact, not long after I lost my summer friend, death was waiting for me once again, lurking just around the corner, ready to take someone else very special from my life.

CHAPTER 5
THIS WAS LIFE
FOR A WHILE

For a brief spell as a child, I experienced at least a passing semblance of normalcy. But, like all things, it didn't last. Still, I can look back fondly on these few years as the time where I finally did learn what it meant to have stability, a sense of home and of place, and most of all...love.

My mother was eventually able to get back on her feet financially with a job that offered decent pay and a chance to climb the corporate ladder, which led to her getting a house she could afford (with the help of her brother, my Uncle Larry). She snatched up my brother and me as quickly as she could and moved us into our new place. The new house was located on Southwood Street in Toledo, and boy, even after all these years, does that street bring a smile to my face. It was in a neighborhood full of kids. I remember long summer days with fireflies and mosquitoes. We would all play outside from early morning until the street lights came on at night. It was just a fun place to live, a place where a child could actually be a child. The stress started to ebb a little bit, and I began to feel what I had been missing for the early part of my life.

Though my mother had gotten us away from our father into the new house, she didn't move there with us as she was still working to get her life back in order. Instead, we lived with Momoo and Dadoo. They were my grandparents on my mother's side who were everything my other grandparents were not. It was absolutely perfect for me and Jason. They were two of the most loving people, everything grandparents should be to their grandkids. I was particularly close with Dadoo. He was so different than my other grandfather, who could be a real jerk. That shouldn't have been a surprise. Like father, like son, I suppose. The apple rarely does fall far from the tree.

The mornings at our house were the best. Every morning, Dadoo would wake Jason and I with a morning back rub. We were his "scorbal-gorgages." Although I was never sure what a scorbal-gorgage was, I sure did love being one. Jason and I then would proceed downstairs to the smell of yummy waffles drenched in butter and syrup for me and butter, peanut butter, and syrup for Jason, which disgusted me! Jason and I had different start times at school, so Dadoo would drive me first, then come home and take Jason. Dadoo had a very old Volkswagen Beetle that was powder blue and had a very distinguished rattling sound that I loved. Driving with Dadoo was always fun. When he would pick us up from school, on approaching the grassy circular area by our house, he would kill the engine and coast into our driveway. Simple and innocent at heart, we thought it was just the coolest thing! This was life for a while and it was absolutely perfect...

Until it wasn't.

In April of 1980, I went on a weekend ski trip to Michigan with my best friend Heather and her father. I loved hanging out with them. Her father was really funny and always made me laugh. I will never forget his motto: "You can never be too rich or too thin." One time, Heather and I went to visit him in Florida during the week of Easter. He picked us up at the airport in his convertible Rolls Royce dressed head to toe in a full bunny costume. I think we acted embarrassed, but we thought it was hysterical! That was the kind of guy he was, and I knew this trip with him and my best friend would be a blast.

When I left that weekend for the ski trip, one of the last things I remember, something that would always stay with me, is my Dadoo cutting me an apple and saltines for a snack. Then he said, "I love you," as he held the door open for me to leave.

That would be my last pleasant memory of him.

The ski trip was just as amazing as I had thought it would be, except for Heather and me showing up late to the car to head home, which made her father pretty angry. It was a quiet and uncomfortable four-hour drive home that was about to get a lot worse.

When we pulled into my driveway, I noticed something was off right away. My mother was dressed up in her work clothes on a Sunday. She came out to the car and exchanged a few words with Heather's dad while I went inside. It was so quiet and nobody was around. I felt panicked. My mother quickly came inside, sat me down, and proceeded to tell me that Dadoo had died of a heart attack. I needed to change my clothes because we had to go to the funeral home.

Shocked doesn't begin to explain how I was feeling. What was worse was that I had no time to process it. I had to go to the funeral home and see him for what would be the last time. I had to look at him in the casket at his showing. That's how I remember him now, a visual too disturbing to share, but enough to know that wasn't my Dadoo in there. When Clint passed, at first I was sad that I didn't take our girls to go see him. But then I remembered how Dadoo looked and I was satisfied with my decision. That's not how I wanted the girls to remember him. That's not how I wanted to remember Dadoo.

I remember my heart hurting so bad in the days and weeks after he passed. I would lie on his side of the bed and pretend he was still there. I would wake up each morning wondering why he wasn't there to give us our morning back rubs. I would think of him every time somebody else took me to school. Dadoo's departure felt like the end of Round Two in my fight to get a normal family life. It was good while it lasted, but still way too short. And things were never really the same again.

Not before too long, Momoo started dating this man named Al. I think she knew him from many years prior, an old friend of sorts. But he was nothing like Dadoo. Granted, he had big shoes to fill, but I don't remember him being very nice or even loving. He had a slight drinking problem and some serious anger issues as well. It felt very foreign when he moved in with us, almost like he was invading on what we had built together.

The whole thing felt off to me. I didn't understand how Momoo could replace Dadoo with Al. She had been with Dadoo most of her life. It just seemed wrong. Of course, I understand better now. There is no replacing. I feel if we are fortunate enough to meet someone we are compatible with, lightning rarely strikes twice. Finding the right person *once* is difficult enough. It is a true blessing to find this twice. Of course, no matter what, it will feel different. You may have to go through an obstacle course to get through all of the different feelings and emotions that will undoubtedly come up. But eventually, hopefully, you will learn to adapt, accept that person for who they are and not who you miss, and realize it's just the next chapter of this great adventure. I believe that sharing life is what makes life worth living. It doesn't need to be anything more than that. We as humans tend to complicate things. It's just sharing our time while we are here with someone who wants to share it too. So we might as well live and find a place of acceptance and happiness.

Still, that's not how the mind of a child works. I didn't like him. I had lost my Dadoo, yet another experience with loss and one that gave me a larger view of how happiness is truly fleeting and nothing lasts forever, especially something you love. That's a tough lesson to learn at an early age, and it's one that would stick with me for years and years, often making me wonder if love was ultimately worth the price. For the record, Momoo and Al were married, but it didn't last long. I guess Momoo chose correctly the first time, and not so much the second time.

One other quick little side note about my experience living with Momoo and Dadoo. It was here that I started to manifest things in my life, where I would *will* them into existence. I believed I had the power to do this. I still do. Too much of what I have willed has come to pass, that I can't ignore it. Say what you will, it works. Or at least it has for me. There is so much truth to the fact that what you pay attention to will grow. You have to make sure whatever you are feeling resonates deep in your soul. You have to think it and feel it, and it has to be truthful. You will know this because it will just feel right. This has been my experience, and it started in that wonderful house in one of the happiest times in my life.

I had a little pink room with a cool walk-in closet. The floor was wood and the ceiling sloped down so you couldn't stand straight up. I remember it smelled strongly of moth balls. It was like my own secret room. In the back, underneath a wood shelf, I kept an imaginary box. It was made of dark brown wood on the outside. The inside was lined with soft black velvet. Nestled inside, in their own little slots, were three big diamond-shaped gems, about the size of a child's fist. The colors were ruby, emerald, and sapphire. The emerald was in the middle because it was my favorite. They were so sparkly, and I kept them well polished! No finger prints were allowed to smudge the surface and take away the beautiful shine they all carried.

I did not actually possess these gems; they were just in my imagination.

For a while.

CHAPTER 6
A SENSE OF SECURITY

When we can't find stability at home--and God knows that was mostly the case with me and my siblings--we tend to look for it elsewhere. For most children, the place that can often establish a solid foundation, help build confidence and life skills, or at least provide an escape from the problems at home is...school.

For *most* children.

Just as I bounced around from home to home, family member to family member in my early years, I also took a rough and tumble journey through the school system, often switching schools and never finding my comfort zone in any of them. I never had time or the opportunity to, and I'm not even sure if it would have made a difference if I had. My experience through grade school didn't help with my sense of feeling lost, though at the time, I didn't even really understand what being lost even meant. I just knew that something about my childhood wasn't right, and jumping from place to place and school to school contributed to that.

While I was at the red house, I went to a school called Fort Miami. My only memory there was walking home from school with these kids we knew and watching a boy my age named Dude try rushing across the street to beat traffic...and not making it. He got hit and ended up in pretty bad shape. Then there was the Lial school while we were at the apartment, then Clarks Lake Elementary when we were with Dad in Michigan, and eventually OLPH when we moved in with Momoo and Dadoo. This was all before the second grade.

OLPH is where the discomfort and sense of instability outside as well as inside the home started. OLPH stood for Our Lady of Perpetual Help. I have to say, I never understood or cared for that name. I always felt it sounded like those of us attending needed extra help. It felt like a special school where they made you feel anything other than special. I heard other names for OPLH...Old Ladies Poor House, or if you were feeling particularly vulgar, Old Ladies Piss House. Now that we were finally settled in one spot, it was decided that I should repeat first grade. Thus began my twelve year journey through the Catholic school system...and my fear of nuns.

Sister Elizabeth is a name that will forever be imbedded in my brain. To me she was the first thing that actually made me fear God. She was our school principal, a deeply devout church traditionalist, and just a *mean* woman. I swear I never saw her smile. Not once.

When I was in second grade, I had to start wearing these special braces on my legs because I walked like a duck with my feet turned out (something that would actually *help* me later in my dancing career). They were awful looking. In addition, I also had these horrid brown and booger-green suede saddle shoes attached to the braces. I had always wanted saddle shoes, but when we had gone shopping for them, the traditional black and white ones were sold out, so brown and booger green it was. While they were in fact helping me fix my legs, needless to say, I was very self-conscious about them.

I remember one time walking down the quiet hall at school and seeing Sister Elizabeth at the other end. I walked toward her to get to class and upon passing her, I looked straight in her eyes. She just glared at me the whole time I walked by her and then she looked at my legs. Not only did she not smile or perhaps say something reassuring, she did nothing. She just stared at me with a terrifying blank glare. I feared her big time, and all she did was add to my insecurity.

She also wanted to paddle me once. I had to go to the office because a boy was pushing me around in a chair in the classroom during indoor recess. As he pushed me, my foot went into a hole in the wall that was already there and made it bigger, and we were sent to the office. Unbelievably, I had to call to get permission for Sister Elizabeth to paddle me, but my mom was pissed and said absolutely not. I think the boy got it though.

It wasn't just Sister Elizabeth. I had a teacher slap me across the shoulder in second grade because I couldn't answer this fill-in-the-blank question in our reading group. I remember it stung, and I cried. These all might not be that big of a deal to some. In fact, they sound like the kinds of things many kids experience growing up, especially in the Catholic school system. But I wasn't a bad kid. I was a deeply emotional kid looking for a safe space, a sense of security, and people and instances like this did nothing but add to my constant sense of discomfort. Add having to go to church and being taught about God and how we should fear Him, how we're all born sinners, and how we have to spend our lives making up for it, and I was filled with constant anxiety and, well, *fear*.

While at school, I wasn't popular or exceptional. I didn't care to be. I just tried my best to get through those early years unscathed. That was one time in my life when I fully agree that ignorance was bliss. It was also during this time that my mother started dating and eventually married my stepfather John Laskey.

My mom worked for John's company, and we knew him and had met some of his kids as well as his wife. In fact, we would sometimes go over to their house to play. However, at some point

John and my mother grew closer and soon they were officially together.

Forget *The Brady Bunch* and *Eight is Enough*. When our families combined, we put them to shame with a total of eleven kids! I always liked to see how fast I could say all the names from oldest to youngest. Kriss, Greg, Steve, Laurie, Gaylene, Michael, Kelly, Bill, Kori, Brett, Jason! His kids at one time or another all went to OLPH. So let me paint a little picture for you. We were two separate families that became one big family belonging to the same parish, at a Catholic school. People talked, and I'm firmly convinced now that this was at least part of the reason I seemed targeted by Sister Elizabeth at the Piss House.

John was so nice, and I was happy for my mom, even at a young age. But it did make our chaotic lives even more chaotic, especially with the introduction of our new stepbrothers and stepsisters. I initially loved all eight kids. They seemed so cool and it was fun at first. In fact, it actually started to feel a bit like a, dare I say it... *family.*

But over the years I began to learn about the animosity and the anger some of them felt about us and I am sure about my mother. Things eventually got back to me. Not that I could blame them. After all, we had broken up their family. I understood that loss of stability more than anyone. They were forced to see their parents separate and to have to welcome this new woman and her three kids into their lives. How messed up is that? I of course didn't understand at the time, but that was when everything started caving in again. What I thought was one thing was really not. Once I became aware of what was being said, or how they felt, I went from thinking we were a happy family to having the sadness, loneliness, and insecurities creeping in again. It was just more of the same.

The one that hurt the most was Bill. He was just a little older them me, and we bonded pretty quickly. I really thought he had my back. He was one grade higher, and as we got older, we would be at the same parties and around the same people. I used to think how cool it was to have a big brother looking out for me. I felt like we had formed a special relationship over the years, but some things he said eventually got back to me. It had to do with some misconceptions about my current relationship, as well as how I acted with my other male friends. He apparently had his thoughts but never once came to me to discuss it. I'm not sure how I would have handled it if he did. Instead of being a protective big brother, he helped spread some rumors that were hurtful, and then things escalated.

It came to a head when we were in high school. We were at a party, and a friend of mine heard him talking about me. They left the room that he was in and came and told me. I cannot remember his exact words but it had something to do with me being a slut. I wasn't, at all, and hearing this from someone I looked at as not just my friend, but my big brother, hurt me deeply. That hurt instantly turned into rage. I literally do not know what came over me but I got in his face about it in front of everyone. He turned his back on me and walked outside and I jumped on him, tackled him to the ground, and started beating him. He refused to fight back, and I bruised and scratched him up pretty good before someone pulled me off of him. I really think I unleashed a lot of anger on him. The next day, as we sat there trying to explain what happened to my mother and his father, I knew our relationship would never be the same.

It wasn't until years later that I would find out that Bill had a secret. He had been hiding the fact he was gay, which I'm sure led to some pent-up frustrations of his own. I can only imagine how hard that was on him. Sadly, we never really recovered from that night. One day quite a few years later, he wasn't feeling well so his roommate took him to the hospital and dropped him off. His family was unaware of this. Next thing he knew, he was going in for a surgery. He never made it out. It was a sad ending, neither of us ever having a chance to express the feelings that kept us apart after our fight. To this day I regret that I never resolved things with him. It's yet another reminder that life is short and we need to let things go.

Between the back and forth of living in Michigan and Ohio, we had to switch schools a lot. This mellowed out when we moved in with Momoo and Dadoo. The last school I ended up at on this whirlwind journey was St. Patrick's of Heatherdowns, where I went with my brother Jason after Dadoo died. I liked the name of this school much better. It made sense to me because it was located on Heatherdowns Blvd. in Maumee, Ohio. It was yet another school with nuns, but my fear had dissipated. I had grown numb to them. Mrs. Kasper was the principal, and to this day I still think of "the friendly ghost" when I hear that name. She wasn't that friendly though. She didn't care for me, mainly because of who I was hanging out with at the time.

And that's why this school is most significant. It's at St. Patrick's where I would meet the one person in my life just as influential as Clint, though not nearly as positive. It's where I would start a lifelong tumultuous journey into obsession, pain, fear, and more... while also finding at least a temporary (if not delusional) sense of stability. All these "losses" that I've addressed over these opening chapters set me up in a vulnerable, if not desperate situation, looking for something to grasp onto, to give me comfort. All of what happened in my early years formed a perfect storm, and I was waiting for it to break. I just needed the right thing to make that happen.

Then I met Cal.

CHAPTER 7
EMBRACING THE
CONFUSION

Cal quite simply took that storm that had been my life and turned it into a monsoon wrapped in a hurricane...and it still hasn't stopped raining.

Cal is the ultimate enigma in my life, in terms of how we connected, why I became so obsessed with him, the effects he's had on me over the years and, despite all the horrible stuff we've been through, how we've still managed to fight for a semblance of a relationship, albeit often a very unhealthy one. Cal and my feelings about him are absolutely and totally confusing, a chaos theory in day-to-day practice. There are not enough therapy session hours that could possibly help me understand our dynamic and why he continues to puzzle, mystify, and in some ways control me still to this day. I have experienced and continue to experience a full range of emotions when I think of, talk about, or occasionally connect with Cal. Love, hate, pity, rage, concern, frustration, fondness, sadness...you name it, they're all there. But one thing is undeniable: he is one of the single most important players in my story and in many ways, the impetus for a lot of what has happened in my life, especially the bad.

Some of this I still struggle with today.

I should actually say right at the start that "Cal" is not his actual name. I don't feel the need to name him. It wouldn't serve any purpose other than to vilify him or bring unwanted drama. Cal has experienced some success in his career, especially as a writer, and when I told him I was going to write about him, he even expressed his fear that this story "would ruin him." Personally, I think that's a little dramatic because we were children during this time, but then again, I'm not on his side of things. I'm also a lot more forgiving than most people, as you'll soon see. I also don't know why I care so much about whether or not this bothers him, but even after everything, I still do. Maybe the fact that I'm still being true to myself, that I'm still caring and thoughtful about him is a testament to the fact that Cal didn't completely change me. I believe, if you don't get to the core of the problem, and process events that happen in your life to the point where you can accept, forgive, and move on, then it is pointless. Or maybe I'm just naïve. Either way, this is the path I'm choosing to take. Besides, when he reads this--and he will--he'll know who he is, and maybe that's all that matters.

The first time I met Cal, I would have been ten years old. We were both on the swim team at Laurel Hill, which was a big swim and tennis club in Toledo. In the summers, Jason and I practically lived there. Back then you didn't need adult supervision, so we would get dropped off at the pool in the morning and essentially stay there all day. I don't recall Cal coming to many swim practices or meets. I just remembered he walked around the place like he owned it. He talked to everyone; he had quite a big personality, and everyone seemed to get a kick out of him. He could hold his own in conversations with adults, and he was very funny. He had this dry sarcasm about him, that if you weren't in tune with him, it would go right over your head. He first noticed me at the club. I'd find out later he thought I was cute, but I didn't really pay him too much attention.

If only it had ended there, but that's not where this particular path leads.

My story with Cal really began in sixth grade. I would like to dedicate the song "The End of Innocence" by Don Henley to this time in my life; a time of changes, feelings, and experiences that came way too soon. When I met Cal, I mean *really* met him, I was a lost little girl, and he was a lost boy. This combination did not work well together.

Sixth grade at a new school was a whole new ball game for me. It was so strange because I started getting attention and the boys, who were exploring new feelings of their own, started to think I was "cute." I remembered thinking, "Me...really?" This was so strange to me. There were three sixth grade classes, and I wasn't even aware this was the school Cal went to, nor was it even a concern in my mind.

On my very first day, I befriended the one girl that talked to me. We were sitting outside at recess, and as I was talking to her, I looked up from my cute little saddle shoes (I had finally gotten my black and white ones!) and walking toward me was Cal surrounded by probably six other boys. We all have those seemingly insignificant moments that turn out to be life-defining. Little did I know that sitting there admiring my saddle shoes was going to be among the final things I ever did as an innocent child.

Cal was popular of course, and still had that blazing wit about him. He was only a year older physically, but mentally he had already been through the ringer. I remember being surprised to see him, and even more surprised that I had a feeling of excitement inside. I also couldn't believe that all of these boys went out of their way to come talk to me. Cal was obviously the one with the idea to walk over. I don't even remember what was said; I'm sure it was simple playground banter, but shortly after this it got back that he liked me.

I couldn't believe it! Why would he like me? Whatever the case, my attention immediately focused on him. He was so cool, so popular, and he didn't seem afraid of or intimidated by anyone. I loved that. I am sure that later in our relationship, this is what made me feel safe. He was in charge, he was in control, he was confident. He was everything I wasn't. I fell head over heels instantly, and that was it.

Remember those cartoons where a villain latches on to his prey with his laser beam eyes and nothing can break it? That is what happened. Nothing was going to come between this bond that was beginning to form. And when it formed, everyone and everything lost out.

Including me.

It started off so innocent. We would talk on the phone for hours. He made me laugh; he showered me with attention and affection; he made me feel so good; he made me happy. He was so interested in me, which was giving me a confidence that a girl who had been bounced around in her family could latch onto. This was what I had been waiting for, and it was amazing!

It was around seventh grade and my sister, who was sixteen, was dating a guy who lived across the street from Cal. She would go to his house, so I would drive along with her and go over to Cal's house. His parents were never really around. This is the time in most lives when we experience new feelings, and we begin to explore those feelings. For some of us, things escalate very quickly...whether we want them to or not.

One day as Cal and I were at his house alone, he pulled me into his dad's closet and taught me how to kiss. I felt weird at first, but he knew what he was doing and I felt so safe with him. I did kind of feel bad, like it was something I shouldn't be doing, but it was exciting too. If it had stayed with that innocent kiss, at least for a little while, things would have been fine.

But it didn't.

Kissing led to touching and fondling and soon onto other

things like oral sex. The first time we had sex was soon after at the indoor tennis courts at Laurel Hill. There were a bunch of them surrounded by huge curtains that went all the way around. As kids, we used to sneak down and run behind them. When the courts were not being used, all the lights were off and it was really dark. We were not supposed to be back there ever...and that was part of the fun! After this particular day, I could never look at those tennis courts or run around down there in the same way again.

I don't know how the conversation came up, but we snuck down there. He first asked me to give him a blowjob. I had already done that for him a few times, and I hated it. So when he asked me if I wanted to have sex instead, I said ok. Whatever he wanted. That's what young love and obsession can lead you to do.

It was short and painful on so many different levels, but it was also something I was doing for the "man" I loved. From then on, we had sex pretty regularly. I would often say I was going to a friend's after school but really I would walk to his house. We would have sex and I would stay for a couple hours then leave.

Even back then, I knew I was making the choice to have sex for him. I didn't really want to, not at all. It felt so wrong. It was a sacrifice on my part, even when doing so made me happy. I only defined my happiness by his happiness...and that was the problem. It also hurt when I would see him flirting with other girls right after we started having sex. Here I was feeling like shit, jealous of all my friends and other girls my age that still had their innocence, and he didn't even seem to care about the sacrifice I was making for him. Because of my obsession, the only thing I thought I could do was try to be more for him.

During the early years, it became apparent to everyone that the scenario was not good. The main objective would be to keep the two of us apart. Friends, teachers, even my mother all gave it a good try. But this bond was not going to be broken that easily. That's what control is, and Cal had all the control. I don't neces-sarily blame Cal; he treated me and loved me the way he was treated and loved, and honestly, he probably didn't know any better. Cal's dad was Middle Eastern and very traditional. He was a hard, disciplined man who was also very chauvinistic. Cal's mom was a scared little mouse who worked all the time at the restaurant they owned. I saw his dad every now and then, though I never got a good feeling from him. His mom was always sweet to me, but seemed pretty clueless as to what Cal was up to, especially later on. Not only did Cal not really ever get any guidance on love, he was essentially on his own from the time he was four. He also experienced a couple of sexual assaults, one from his stepbrother and another from a swim coach that had taken him camping. He was a scared boy who carried around a lot of anger...and he needed an outlet.

See, even all these years later, I still do that. I still make excuses for him. That's power.

I wish I could explain how I allowed him to have full control over me. He told me he loved me, and that was all I wanted. Really, that was at the heart of it. In the instability of my younger years, I didn't feel loved and he loved me. I was willing to do anything to hang onto that. I would soon learn that he was not capable of the love that I was so longing for, but what the hell do we know about love that early on? Plus, the fear of losing him was always present. He was all I had, especially when it came to men in my life. My father didn't give a shit. Dadoo was gone. My stepfather had so many kids of his own to focus on. I would do whatever it took to keep Cal. Unfortunately, it came at the cost of losing myself.

I soon became his puppet. This started with Cal but continued to follow me through my life. I had such low self-esteem, I didn't realize I had choices. I was always too afraid to voice my feelings, even if I was totally against something, or didn't want to do something. The whole time, something inside me would be so angry that I wasn't standing up for myself. That's the worst part; being a puppet, knowing you're a puppet, and not having the strength to do a damn thing about it.

After we started having sex, Cal began to change. He started being mean and more forceful. He seemed angry, and he took it out on me. It became less about him loving me and more about him threatening me. He knew I was scared of losing him, and I think he got a kick out of seeing how far he could get me to go and what he could get away with. He started telling me about other girls who were so beautiful and so nice and who would do anything for him. So if I wanted to keep him, I had to do what he wanted.

We had sex more often and in different places. Sex became more of a guilty thing, especially as I felt the pressure of my Catholic upbringing. I felt dirty and used, not sweet and innocent like the other girls in my class, none of whom were as sexually active as me. All of this just added to the feelings of unworthiness and insecurity. I also soon realized that what I thought was sacred and between him and I was clearly a bad assumption on my part. I started hearing all sorts of rumors about Cal with other girls. This was the most difficult because I felt so full of shame.

My so-called friends and extended family would tease me about it, and even my stepfather John called it out once. "You act like you're so innocent, but we know better." He had a smile on his face, and I remember how much pain I was in. I know he didn't even mean anything by it. How would he know I was keeping this as my own shameful secret? But I felt like this was how everyone was looking at me. This was not me. I wasn't enjoying having sex. I was doing it to keep Cal and for no other reason. I never even had an orgasm with him. I didn't even know what an orgasm was back then. It was all about him. Well into my adult life, I would hold back from having an orgasm when in a serious relationship because if I did have one this major guilt would set in, like it was wrong for me to feel good. That even carried into my relationship with Clint. I had so many hang-ups about it, even with a man who loved me completely.

One time we were walking through the woods and Cal picked up this long, thin branch and began hitting me with it. It felt like a whip. He was laughing so I was laughing to, but then it began to really hurt. I was confused why he was hitting me with it, but it hurt so I started running...fast. He was running after me, and he caught up and hit me with it again. I ran again and I got scared and started screaming. But no one was around, and I couldn't run anymore. I stopped, and he caught up. Even though I asked him not to hit me, the next one hit my eye. I started crying, and he said he was sorry, but it didn't feel sincere.

I could tell he liked it.

It only got worse. I remember a particular time when I was thirteen. I snuck out to be with Cal. His friend was having a party and eventually we ended up in someone's bedroom. We were lying in bed together and the room was dark. I heard the door open, and someone walked in. I had seen him at the party earlier and although I personally didn't know him, I knew of him. He was nineteen years old and was quite the bully. He loved picking fights and nobody liked to mess with him. When he saw us, he climbed into the bed, and Cal instantly climbed out and left the room. I was then told by this bully that I had two choices: I could either have sex with him or I could give him oral sex. Feeling trapped, abandoned, and terrified, I chose sex. I remember just lying there and crying. When he was done, I got myself together and went looking for Cal. He was nowhere to be found. Unfortunately, since I had told my mother I was staying at a friend's house, and I had been dropped off by my stepbrother, I didn't have a ride home. I actually stayed the night. In the morning, the only way of getting home was from the guy who raped me the night before.

I thanked him for the ride.

I also never got an explanation or anything about this from Cal, at least, not at the time.

In some ways, I started to become numb. But desperation and obsession also had me screaming on the inside. All I wanted was his love and acceptance. I was so sad, I needed him to love me. He was all I had. Couldn't he see what he was doing to me and how I was hurting? Did he not care at all?

The answer was no. Not really.

He liked all girls, and he wanted and needed a lot of attention. Just because I was there for him to do whatever he wanted, it didn't really make a difference. I wasn't special. I had given myself to him thinking I was. I continued to do so to keep him, and he began to play the mental games.

During eighth grade, Cal got kicked out of school for fighting. He ended up going to a public school, and when I graduated, I went to Central Catholic, which made him mad. I knew once we were separated, things would fade, and I was crushed. Although we drifted apart in high school, the painful feelings were still there. First, it was of losing him, but soon after, it turned to anger. Not being around him regularly gave me time to really think and process the emotions I had been bottling up. I began to realize he never cared about me and that didn't just make me sad, it filled me with rage. For his birthday one year, I took every note, gift, or whatever I had from him or about him, wrapped it in a box, and left it at his house. I thought it might give me some closure. It didn't come close. The things that happened between us and the aftershocks ran deep and were not going to go away anytime soon.

And yet...we've stayed in touch over the years. I honestly don't know why. I really don't. When we were working on this chapter, my editor said he was going to "embrace the confusion" when it came to my writing about Cal and maybe that's what I really need to do. Because it is confusing. Over the years I have had a multitude of feelings regarding him. I still love him in many ways. But how can I continue to be compassionate to somebody who hurt me? What he did was horrible. Or maybe it's not his fault. Maybe that's just what he knew. Why the hell would I make excuses for him? He's a terrible person. Or maybe he's just lost. I'm worried about him. I really want nothing to do with him. I hope he's ok. I wonder if he ever still thinks of me. Fuck him. Why does he still have a hold on me? Why are we still friends? I hope what I write here hurts him. Or maybe helps him? I want nothing but the best for him. Do I care? Does he care?

Embracing the confusion.

Cal is going to pop up several more times in this story, typically at times when I'm at my weakest and most vulnerable. I need to be clear that, despite my mixed emotions, I don't blame him for everything. And I do believe that there is good in him, regardless of his overwhelming ego, one that he still embraces today. There was some good in him back when we were just kids trying to find something to hold. We had a bond, and that is undeniable. Even if it was built a bit on delusion, at least on my end, it was still a connection and an impactful one. As sad as it is, he was my first love and we never forget our first. We were both lost, hurt, and broken when we met. Although it didn't go well, we were both fueled by something more. We both had our own struggles over the years but we made it out and both succeeded in our own ways. There will always be a connection. The bond is deep for that reason, and perhaps that reason alone.

Unfortunately, when I was a child, I had put all of my eggs in the Cal basket. That's not a mistake I would make today, but I was younger and so much more desperate then. Sadly, this person, this particular kind of love, didn't help me solve the problems I was facing and feeling from the many losses in my life. If anything, it just made me feel more loss and I soon began to realize there was nothing in my life that I could control. And that's what I needed more than anything else, really. I needed something to tether me to reality, to make me feel something good, to give me some power and stability.

The problem is, that as a child, and as I had proven with Cal, we will look for those things anywhere and we'll take it wherever we can find it, even in the worst of places and the most harmful of choices.

CHAPTER 8
I FELT CLEAN

"You cannot change what you refuse to confront." – John Spence

I love quotes. I love how some very wise or, if you will, highly enlightened humans can come up with such profound messages in so few words. I feel if we are open and aware, these powerful words can have quite an impact on our life.

With this one, I could not agree more. We have to get to the source of the problem. Otherwise these problems will keep manifesting in different areas and in different ways in our life. It's almost like changing costumes in a performance. If you don't know the choreography, it doesn't matter what costume you have on...you still don't know the choreography! You cannot perform at your highest potential unless you do.

In its simplest form, if something is bothering us, no matter how big or how small, we have to get to the root of the problem and allow ourselves to understand the "why" or the "what" in order to process the issue. Then, and only then, can we let go. This is very difficult work and we have to be willing to do that work or the process is pointless. It's taken me many years to do this work, to even just start the processing of all the "junk" tucked deep inside me that has manifested itself time and time again throughout my life. I'm obviously still working through this, which is partially why I'm writing this book.

For many years, I refused to face something that has been a problem for most of my life. Even when I did acknowledge and accept it, I refused to confront it, to examine where it came from, so I could (potentially) beat it. The guidance of an incredible therapist—along with my own self-reflection—has helped me start to dig and to get some clarity on where this particular issue came from and why it's been such a huge presence through good times and especially, the bad. I'm just now starting to understand, even as I still struggle to fight it. Even just saying it out loud, admitting to what it really is and how long it's been there, is still difficult. I know there will be some people reading this, some very close to me, who will be surprised by this, even if they've occasionally had their suspicions. Not everybody, but some. But if this book is going to do what I need it to do, to help me find some clarity and catharsis and avoid going down the rabbit hole once again, I have to put my truth out there as best as I can. I need to expose all of me, to share, to reflect, to grow.

I need to confront, so I can change.

For most of my life, from the time I was in junior high on, I've struggled with an eating disorder. I've hid it as best as I can from those who have loved me most, including my husband and children. I've let it absolutely control me throughout periods of my life, especially the difficult ones. It has led to other horrible decisions and dangerous mistakes. And, perhaps hardest to admit, despite how well I'm doing, I still struggle with it today.

Which is why I need to look at it, and look hard.

It's hard to pinpoint exactly when it started. I cannot remember a time in my life where I sat down to eat anything and did not have guilt and anxiety about it. It makes me so sad to think of the time spent obsessing over that anxiety and guilt, almost hourly. What a waste of mental power. As a child, anxiety and guilt were just a part of my daily life. With all the losses I experienced and my constant need for stability, this was something I maybe thought I could control. I'm pretty sure the seeds of this eating disorder were always there, just waiting in the soil for someone to water them.

My unhealthy obsession with Cal proved to be all it needed to start growing.

Now, I need to be clear as I don't want to blame my eating disorder on anyone but myself. Cal didn't make this happen; it was always there and I believe it was going to happen no matter what. It was just a matter of time. But the circumstances of our relationship, combined with my lack of stability and my need for control, created a perfect storm.

The first incident I can remember where I really started to think of controlling what I ate came when I saw one of the other girls that Cal was dating. She was very pretty, and I noticed her hipbones stuck out. As odd as this sounds, for some reason, this appealed to me. I don't know why it had such an impact. I was very thin as it was, and yet, I wanted to look like her. That's how it really started. From that moment on, I developed an eating disorder that would affect everything in my life, becoming a constant presence.

It is absolutely unbelievable how much we allow the voices inside our head to run our lives. Why are we so mean, so damaging to ourselves? Where does this come from? Low self-esteem, guilt, shame, and anger plagued me for many years. I spent so much time in my head, listening to a bully. I spent so much time believing I couldn't do anything, believing I was less then everyone, and wanting to be something else better than myself. I wanted to be noticed, and if being thin would make that happen, then that is what I wanted to be. All I wanted was love and acceptance, especially from Cal. I was so sad. I needed him to love me, as I felt like he was all I had. I was hurting and lost and needed something to shift. By the time I entered high school I was leading sort of a double life, for lack of better words. There was the girl I was, and the girl I wanted to be. I hid my insecurities very well, but I was so envious of strong girls. I would have done anything to have had their confidence. How did they know how to be like this? Was it taught to them? Were they born like that? Once I saw the girl Cal was with, for whatever reason, that was the trigger that brought all this to the surface and the idea evolved. If I couldn't control my surroundings, my circumstances, or my feelings, I would find something I could control.

So food, or lack thereof, became my obsession. From there on out everything revolved around me obsessing over how little I could eat. I remember very well the first time I held back from eating for two days. I felt so good, so strong that I could do that. It was strange really, I felt so proud of myself. I felt *clean.* When hunger finally forced me to eat a piece of toast, I was immediately consumed with guilt. I was so angry that I gave in! There were always those times of weakness. I would want to eat, so I would. Then the guilt, the pain, the shame would set in. I lost the control. It was these times that would send me in a downward spiral. The voices in my head were getting stronger and stronger, and eventually they took control.

You have to get rid of it. You feel dirty and disgusting. Get rid of it! I won't let you stop thinking about this until you do! It will all disappear and you will feel clean and you will be in control again!

So once, I did. That was it. That one time was all it took. This began my very long battle with bulimia. Purging gave me the sense of control I had been looking for all along.

First thing you must know, having this particular kind of eating disorder is work. So for me, I had to make it worth it. I realized it was more satisfying if there was something to purge. So not eating, and then eating something small was not enough. To put myself through that, I would have to have more food in me. I never really went as far as binging, but I would have to have the feeling of fullness. If I was sad or something shifted my emotions, it would trigger the voice.

Ok, you are not feeling good. You are feeling sad or angry or out of control. You want to feel better and you will feel better after you purge, so eat a little more. Might as well enjoy some food that you normally wouldn't eat. Then get rid of it!

I would eat, then go to the restroom, stick my finger down my throat, and breathe in. Then it would happen. At first it was difficult; my stomach muscles and chest would be sore. It took time and practice, but I got used to the technique, making sure to do it a few times so everything came up. I've heard some others describe this as a euphoric sensation. I never once felt peace or a sense of euphoria. It was hideous, shameful, and gross. I hated it! That being said, when it was done, I felt clean and relieved to have that power to make myself feel good again.

I also gained power from it by hiding it. When I started my eating disorder, I didn't look that much different. I was skinny but not anorexic. This is difficult to say, but I was envious and in awe of anorexics because I was amazed at the control they had. I never had that much control.

I got pretty good at planning how to adhere to my disease. If I was upset or feeling in need of a purge, I knew where I would have to be and when a good time would be. That part wasn't hard and even if and when it was, it was worth it.

And yes, I felt hungry a lot, but this was fine because I believed it allowed me to not feel anything else. The eating disorder was my own self-inflicted punishment as well. It was my punishment for not standing up for myself, for not being worthy. Punishing myself in this way also led me to those feelings of control. It's hard to explain, but it really did feel at the time that it was the ultimate solution to everything I was feeling. In fact, remember early on when I mentioned those awful migraines I used to get? Well, vomiting always magically took the pain away.

I became full blown bulimic. Bulimia is such an ugly word. I hated all of this with a passion and I definitely knew it was a problem, even back when it started. But I felt helpless. I felt so defeated all the time. Like any kind of addiction, it was powerful. And terrifying. I read so much about what it can do to the body, especially the physical stress, and I even wondered if it could cause me to eventually have a heart attack. I knew what I was doing was horrible for me. I had the awareness, but that need for control, that constant search to fill the void and numb myself from the sadness and pain, was too powerful.

It hasn't gone away, not completely. Even though I have my eating disorder contained, all those feelings and the memory of how it made me feel, are still there. So are the voices. I am not over this disease, and I don't know if I ever truly will be. Through the years, it became relevant in my career as a dancer. There was a time that my weight fluctuated, and it got more difficult as I got older. When I was heavier I was always so depressed, so I would control it and it consumed me. I've tried so hard at different times in my life to help myself kick this disease. I wanted to not have this be a problem, but I just couldn't fathom how that could happen. I bought books, I did research, but to no avail. In fact, there was one time I was so desperate, I found a therapist in Vegas and had a session with him. I literally bared my soul, wanting him to be able to give me something, anything that would give me hope that this could go away. His last words to me were, "Try not to throw up until the next time I see you." I was in shock, totally deflated. After that I was like, "Fuck it, I tried."

It also continued into my marriage to Clint and that pains me more than anything. I lied to him for many years, hiding it from him. He knew about it (or some of it, at least) early on and tried to help in his own way, but I continued to hide it from him over the years. It was easy to keep all this a secret because he worked so much at night. The purging would only get bad if I couldn't keep on a strict food intake. I felt even more guilt and shame for not letting this man who loved me in on my terrible secret. Maybe he could have helped me, given me the strength to get help and kick it once and for all. I know he loved me so much he would have been willing to fight alongside me. But I never gave him the chance. I never shared this pain with him. I think I was too afraid to lose this control. When he died it spiraled out of control because my life was out of control.

Clint hasn't been gone long, and I can still hear those voices whispering. I cringe when I think about how much time in my life I have wasted on this. I hate that I even have to bring it up, to admit to those who love me and anyone reading this that I've been hiding this for all these years, along with the pain it's caused. But I have to be honest, especially as it lays the groundwork for some of what comes next in my story. I also need to be honest in order to confront it.

"You cannot change what you refuse to confront."

CHAPTER 9
CHICKERY CHICK

Sometimes we find what we're looking for in the most unexpected of places.

Amidst everything that happened in my young life--the divorce, the moving around, the death, Cal, my eating disorder--there were of course moments of levity and light. There were good times, moments that I felt whole, stable, and happy. They were often fleeting, but they existed and thank God they did as they were all I had to grasp onto when things started to inevitably go bad. As I searched for more and more of those moments, hoping to find them in my family, my relationship, and even just my own personal journey, I found that most of the stability, joy, and peace I did find revolved around one thing:

Dancing.

Little did I know just how important to my life dancing would eventually become, especially with how it started.

When I was just a child and living at the red house, I was invited by my babysitter Pam to see her two young sisters perform in their dance recital. I had never been to one and didn't know what to expect. I sat in the audience very curious to see what was going to unfold. When the curtain opened, and there were Missy and Debbie along with nine other girls, I was mesmerized.

They were standing center stage in the most beautiful sparkly yellow chick costumes. On top of their heads they had yellow hats with orange beaks attached. On their feet were these awesome shiny black patent leather tap shoes. To a young child, they looked glorious! The number they did was called "Chickery Chick." In all my four years or so of life, this was the most amazing thing I had ever seen! At that very moment, a very large seed was planted in my mind: One day that would be me on stage.

Still, as excited as I was about the spectacle I had witnessed, it took me almost another decade to actually try out dancing. Why it took so long I'm not even really sure, but it could have been because of all the moving around and just the general chaos of life at the time. I didn't have much time for extracurricular activities as a kid. To be honest, I never even really thought about signing up for dance...until I was fourteen.

I will never forget the day my mother asked if I wanted to take dance class. Bam...just like that, a light bulb went off in my head! The memories of sitting in the audience watching the dance recital all came flooding back and I remembered not only how happy it made me, but how excited I was by the idea of being up on a stage. At fourteen, the thought of "Chickery Chick" didn't excite me as much, but I was curious to see what I could learn. She signed me up to take dance class at O'Connell Dance Studio in Toledo, and I was so excited. Unfortunately, that came to a quick and screeching halt during the first class when I realized...

I was horrible.

I was put in a beginner's class, having no prior experience. That meant most if not all of the kids were younger than me. On top of that I was tall, very tall for my age and not very flexible. I just remember looking very uncoordinated. I don't even think I could count the music. In fact, I *know* I couldn't. Everything was just so incredibly awkward, and I didn't have a clue what I was doing. The only thing I did have was a good natural turnout from my misshapen legs. Thank God those awful leg braces never worked out!

I was so embarrassed at my first recital. My first dance I ever performed was to the song "P.Y.T. (Pretty Young Thing)" by Michael Jackson. I remember feeling ridiculous as I was a head or two taller then everyone. My dance teacher put me on the end closest to the wing, almost behind the curtain. Need I say more? To make matters worse, it was at that dance recital that I saw the girl with the hipbones. The one that Cal liked and I emulated. I can still remember watching her perform from behind the curtain. She was so good in these advanced dance numbers that were so cool. The whole thing was a disaster.

But...I didn't quit.

What is crazy is I actually didn't let that experience take me down, not for one second. This was very unlike me. Normally a train wreck like this would have been enough to force me to walk away. But there was something different about dance. I wanted to do this more than anything. I was completely determined to figure it out.

That summer, while my studio was closed, I found another studio to take class. My mom cleared space in our basement and put up some mirrors so I could practice. I started watching *Flashdance*, *Footloose,* and *Girls Just Want to Have Fun* over and over and over. I watched anything with dancing, except for live performances, ironically enough. I couldn't stand being in the audience. I wanted to be up on stage!

I had my brother Mike take me to a dance wear shop where I bought my first pointe shoes. That was funny in itself because I knew nothing about these types of shoes. I was really embarrassed to buy them because the woman selling them was asking me questions about the type I needed, what they were for, and even about the lamb's wool I needed to cover my toes. I didn't have a clue about any of this. I didn't even know how to put them on correctly! I just thought they were so *pretty*. I would have done anything to be a ballerina. That was my favorite kind of dance and what I dreamed of doing up on stage. Although it was a pipe dream, I would stay up at night and watch *Swan Lake*. I was so envious of those dancers, and even though I knew I would never dance like them, I could at least try to look like them physically. I would go to the basement and spend hours trying to get up en pointe. Dance became my passion, despite my struggles, and I never stopped practicing. Once the new season at my studio started, I begged for the instructors to move me up a level, mainly so I could get over my embarrassment of dancing with a bunch of young kids. After major hesitation, they agreed.

Something clicked.

I got better. All the practice, the determination, and those late nights watching the pros do it paid off. I started to feel the music, I could learn the steps easier and even more important, execute them. I got more comfortable in my body (at least while I was dancing) and learned how it could move. Dancers feel something take over when they're on the stage, and I started to experience that. I fell in love with it. From that point on, dance was all I ever wanted to do.

For as troubled as I was as a child and teenager, the escape was like no other. Everything just disappeared while I was dancing. Even my obsession with Cal was put on the back burner when I danced. It wasn't gone, of course, but it allowed me a little freedom from it, a temporary and much-needed reprieve. All I wanted to do was perform. I looked forward to it and the happy feelings it gave me because I felt like I had nothing else that could compare. I was a big fish in a small pond, so for a short time I even developed some confidence and comfort.

Still, being this involved in dance did leave open the door for both danger and disappointment, especially for someone as impressionable and desperate for stability as me. For as much as happiness it brought me, it also contributed to some devastating life choices, which began while I was in high school. It also led to one of the more heartbreaking moments in my strained relationship with my father.

I gave him so many chances and continued to do so in high school. Over the years when we reconnected--or rather, when I reached out to him--I thought for sure this would be the time that our relationship would hold. He was always so convincing and seemed like he wanted it as badly as I did, but he never followed through.

One of the most damning moments in our relationship came when I invited him to my dance recital. The tickets cost $4.75 and I wanted him to see me perform so badly. Sad to say, I was afraid that if I told him he had to buy a ticket, he wouldn't come. I had a feeling that I was not worth him spending that amount of money. I was in a conundrum. I didn't want to ask my mother for the money because I would have felt bad if she knew it was to buy his ticket. I ended up finding the money myself to purchase the ticket. The day of the recital I was so excited. I just knew he would be so proud of me. I went out to meet him in the lobby about an hour before the show. I was hoping to show him the program and point out when I would be on stage.

He wasn't there. That's ok, I thought. It was still early. I left and came back fifteen minutes later. Still no sign. I did that four more times. I waited until the last possible second before I had to be backstage. Although I was bummed I had missed him, I figured he had already gone in and sat down. Once the show began, I peeked into the audience any chance I got. I assumed he was way in the back. While I was performing, I could barely handle the excitement because I knew he was watching. I just knew he would be so proud. When the show ended, I ran out to the lobby as quickly as I could. I couldn't wait to see him. But I still couldn't find him. At the time, I convinced myself that he had been there, but he probably had somewhere to be.

As time went on, I knew better.

Still, the occasional disappointment wasn't enough to dampen my spirits or take away the one positive thing I truly loved in my life. I began to wonder if it could provide me with an opportunity. I was too young to really think about it as a career or something that could make me money, but I knew it was something I loved to do and I couldn't see myself giving it up. Ever. It had filled a very large hole in my life, one I had been looking to fill for quite some time. It gave me focus, confidence, passion, stability, and most important, an escape.

The only problem with escaping from your life is that eventually, you need to come back. And I had many, many troubles waiting for my return.

CHAPTER 10
SLEEP

In retrospect, looking back on what had happened and *was* happening, perhaps this night was inevitable.

We all have a breaking point, even those of us who struggle to keep up a positive demeanor, those of us who care for the world with all our heart, those who simply want the basics in life, most of all love. If the pressure continues to build, if life's disappointments keep landing blow after blow, and we're not in the best place physically, mentally, and even *soulfully*, how can we possibly hold it all in or hold it all together? If you've spent your whole young life feeling lost, looking for something that seems elusive, and you latch on to whatever you can find, no matter how harmful, just to feel something other than loss, you will reach that breaking point. It will mark you in some way for the rest of your life. Even as time passes and heals, you will remember what you once were capable of...and you will always wonder if you're capable of doing it again.

When I was junior in high school, I finally saw the eye of the storm.

While the part of me that had hope and promise focused on

the discipline required to train and maintain the early stages of a possible dance career, there was the rest of me. The lost wanderer, the obsessed and neglected girlfriend, the self-conscious bulimic, the hopeless cherub always looking for but never finding love or a sense of place. On top of that, I was a teenager, which meant, I was all this while living in a time of experimentation. Our teen years are when most of us play with things to make us feel good or at least numb the pain.

I had a lot of pain.

The first time I experimented with drinking was at a big family party. My cousins lived on a farm so there was a lot of land, and everyone was spread out. I really don't know what gave me the idea (or the balls) at nine years old to sneak some beer and drink it, I just remember doing it. If memory serves me correctly, I drank three red cups filled to the rim. The last time filling it, I dropped it, and I was scared because I didn't want to get caught. But I also couldn't stop laughing. The drive home was hard because I was trying to act normally, though I am pretty sure it was obvious. I drank a lot in junior high. One of my close friends had a mother who was never home, so there was a lot of partying at her place. I drank beer, vodka, shots of Jack Daniels chased with water, and even Goldschlager. And like most teenagers, I did some pretty stupid things I don't need to share, things I can look back on and be grateful that I didn't get caught or worse. We all have those, right?

The problem with my drinking is that alcohol is a depressant, and I was already depressed. The voices in my head never stopped, especially when it came to Cal. Did he even care? Did I ever mean anything to him? I was so confused. I just felt so used and worthless. Maybe if I were skinnier? I was sad all the time and soon my sadness turned to anger. Looking to numb myself, I drank more.

I started smoking pot in junior high as well, mainly because I was told it would relax me, which it did. By the time I got to high school, I loved to get high, loved the escape of feeling numb.

The first time I tried cocaine, I was a junior. I would have done anything to get my hands on that. It was such a quick fix to feel complete bliss, but it never lasted. Luckily I didn't have the connection or know how to get it. I had to rely on friends to share from time to time, and I would look forward to those times the most. My favorite song by Pink Floyd was "Comfortably Numb" and my favorite line in the song was "Just a little pin prick..." I wanted to feel like what they were describing in the song. I fantasized about it. I did not know how to deal with these feelings and all the noise and clutter in my head. I constantly craved escape and when I wasn't on stage, this was where I could find it.

But as everyone who has ever used drinking or getting high as a way to escape can tell you, it doesn't last. When it's over, things appear worse than ever. As I went through high school, my overwhelming sadness manifested in a number of different ways, most notably rage. Some could even argue violent rage. And there was nobody I hurt worse than myself.

When I was seventeen, I cut myself for the first time. I was angry at a lot of things, but mainly myself, and I needed a release. I would get to a place of anger where there was no coming back. There was no way of calming myself down. My rage wouldn't allow it. It scared me when I got to this point. I always had quite the temper, and my family still jokes about my freakish strength that comes with that anger. I punched things, threw things, broke things. I just wanted the anger out.

I didn't cut myself how most cutters did it. Honestly, back then I had never heard there was a thing such as cutting. It was just something that I had to do, and it happened one day in a fit of rage. I scratched myself. Hard. And I kept scratching as if I could literally scratch this rage out of me. Suddenly seeing blood would snap me out of it. I felt pain, and that overtook the anger. I would calm immediately because the anger was released and now I could breathe. I looked at the blood and felt...satisfied. Then of course, I faced the problem of trying to hide what I had done. I wasn't smart enough to do this on my legs where the scratches would have been hidden. I did keep my wrists covered, but looking back, maybe I wanted someone to see. One time someone at school actually noticed and they thought I should know that if you are trying to kill yourself you are supposed to slit the vein lengthwise, not across. But this was after I started cutting regularly. When I couldn't cut, I would use what I had on me, most notably my nails. If I was feeling anger in the moment I would grab behind my neck, right under my hair line, and press all my nails into my skin in the center and drag them around the side, to the front, and down my neck. It looked like claw marks and it hurt enough to give me release. Luckily turtle necks were in back then. I wore them a lot.

The drinking, the drugs, the cutting, not to mention the eating disorder all started to become regular parts of my life, of me. The lows that followed each of these just kept adding to my depression, sadness, and anger. As did Cal and my confusion over where we stood, if anywhere at all. Quite literally, I was heartbroken with life.

I knew it was getting bad when I started skipping dance. I was very close with the owner of my dance studio, my teacher Joanie. I recall writing her a letter of apology for not showing up one day. I never took my bad actions easily, still don't. That was another bit of extra pressure, my guilt for what I was doing. In the letter I said how I wished I could just disappear sometimes. I used to think of different scenarios of how I could do it. I wanted to think of a way that it wouldn't look like it was on purpose because I didn't want to hurt my mom or really anyone. I thought about running out in front of a car to make it look like an accident. Where I lived, there wasn't much around but a lot of trees and a long, winding road with nothing around so people would drive fast. Having a plan actually made me feel better.

But wait a minute, what about the driver of the car? How awful would that be for them?

That was just one of many, many scenarios I daydreamed about when I was feeling the lowest. I did see my therapist off and on over my childhood and into my teen years. During elementary school, I spent a lot of time in his office counting the books on his bookshelf. I answered his questions vaguely. No way was he going to get anything out of me. But then there was always the dreaded stare down, where he gave me space and waited patiently for me to open up. I refused. So we locked eyes, and the countdown in my head began. One one thousand, two one thousand, three one thousand... It was actually a good day if I got to three. I slowly lowered my gaze to his beard. Damn, he won again! Then irritation set in.

I liked my therapist. He seemed like a gentle man. That was all I really wanted anyway. I took a couple years off from seeing him, but I asked to go back my junior year and saw him here and there into high school. Honestly, I had nowhere else to go, especially at a Catholic high school. Oh, there was confession, but that was a fucking joke. Did anyone tell the truth? I would have loved to have been a fly on the wall in that phone booth. So therapy helped me try to shake my inner voices.

But I didn't ever really give him enough. I liked hanging out there, but I never really opened up. That didn't stop me from demanding his time and attention. One session, he actually got me to open up, and I said something that alarmed him. I don't remember what, but he got very serious and started talking to me about addressing the issue or he was going to have to get my mom involved. He essentially gave me the option of either me telling her what I was feeling or him doing it. That triggered me. He had to step out for something and I got pissed, so I took off. In itself, that wouldn't seem like a big deal, but because of what happened just a few days later, I've always felt bad about it.

There was a moment in high school, one that I will never forget, one that changed my life forever, and it started just like any other for me in that time of my life. I was at my friend's house, and we were up late partying. Everyone must have been passed out except me and this guy. I don't remember much about him, but I think he was dating my friend Renee, whose house we were at. We decided to leave, just the two of us, and we ended up coming to my Momoo's apartment as I was watching her cat while she was gone.

I was supposed to go home to look after my little brother, who w as just twelve and home alone. Mom and John had flown to Florida because of an emergency with John's father. Everything was a mess and torn up at our house because they were adding onto it. It was a big house on the top of a hill surrounded by a forest.My brother was young and scared and wanted me there.

I left him alone.

This guy and I hung out at the apartment, and I was filled with tremendous guilt over leaving with him. Nothing happened between us, and I asked him to leave before it did. I was so ashamed of myself, wondering how I could do that to my friend Renee. Everything just came to a head. I was so angry and sad and confused and just fucking tired. I wanted to numb the pain... permanently.

I contemplated drinking Drano first. I know how crazy that sounds, but I had just heard that someone had done it that way. I had the bottle open, and was wondering how that would work. Just the smell of it seemed too painful, and I couldn't go through with it. As I fought through (or perhaps succumbed to) the voices screaming in my head and the rage building up inside me, I went to Momoo's medicine cabinet. I took everything that was in it, not knowing what any of it was. I was under the assumption that I could take a bunch of pills, lie down, and just go to sleep. That's how it would happen. It would be peaceful, clean, and easy.

I swallowed as many pills as I could...and quickly realized only *sleeping* pills would give me the peaceful forever slumber I wanted.

I immediately felt like I was wired. My heart was pounding so fast, and I got scared because I wasn't sure what was happening. I started to vomit as my body rejected all of the meds. I started to panic and called some hotline. I was somehow connected to

911, and an ambulance was sent. From there, things happened very fast, and combined with the drinking and the effects of the medicine, it all quickly became a blur.

I remember the paramedics showing up; the cat getting out; one of the paramedics scolding me; them getting the cat back in the apartment; a loud and uncomfortable ride to the hospital; the horrific sensation of nurses pumping my stomach; seeing my aunt and uncle arrive and wondering how they knew; and then...

Sleep.

Regret.

Loss. Loss of whatever innocence I had left.

More sadness, pain, fear, anger.

A life forever altered and––

Wait. Just wait.

I need to take a second to stop looking at the past and wonder about my present, or at least about my most recent life history. I mentioned earlier that we all have these defining life moments, these pieces of time where everything that has happened and is happening to us, all the emotions that go with it and all the influences and circumstances come to a head and change us forever. This suicide attempt when I was in high school was one of those moments, and as you'll soon see, my life did change dramatically.

And yet, as I look at my current life, I wonder how far removed I am from all of these thoughts and feelings, especially in the wake of Clint's sudden and tragic death. Oh, I know I'm not suicidal or anything anymore. But if I'm really being honest, over the past few years, that sadness, frustration, longing, and rage have shown their ugly faces again. As have some of the outlets I used to release, to cover, to conceal, to numb. My life changed all those years ago, and yet my struggles, though in a different shape, often appear the same. I don't know if that is an empowering or terrifying prospect. Empowering in the sense that I have an awareness of it now and am constantly working on it, to avoid going back down that hole and doing things that could hurt me and those that love me, as well as those that rely upon me. Terrifying in knowing that despite everything, including the passage of time *and* that aware-ness, it's all still there, even if it's being held at bay. Maybe it's just waiting for another breaking point to all come flooding out again. Clint's death was about the closest I've come to that next breaking point...and I'm still working as hard as I can at surviving. It hasn't been easy, but I'm here and I'm fighting.

Maybe that's all I can do. Maybe those things are so deeply entrenched in me, so much a part of me, that I'll never fully be able to let them go. Even as I lead a very happy life that's now full of love, joy, comfort, and even that stability I craved for so long, I have to accept those remnants are still there. They're a part of me.

As I continue this journey of looking back to help me with my present, I must go forth with that awareness, to know who I was, who I am, and who I want to be, and to never forget just how bad it got, how I handled it, and how that changed me forever.

CHAPTER 11
IS IT JUST OVER NOW?

I didn't want to die.

I may have thought that I did, but I know enough about myself to know that if I had really wanted to kill myself, I would have. I was hurting and seemed out of options, so I cried out in a very dramatic way. I wanted someone to notice because I didn't know how to speak about how I was feeling. I was too ashamed of everything. As bad as I felt in that moment I swallowed those pills, it didn't compare to how I felt when the ordeal was over...

After my meal of charcoal and the induced vomiting that followed, I was empty and could do nothing more than fall asleep. For how long, I don't know, but it was the sleep of someone exhausted with it all. When I did finally peel my eyes open, I wasn't sure of the time, but I noticed it was still dark. I felt awful and instantly guilty, wondering what I had done and why I had taken things so far. I think I knew even in that moment, that first moment I awoke, that there would be consequences to my actions.

And that I would never be the same again.

I glanced across the room and found my mom and John sitting

in the chairs. The only thing I could think of was how had they gotten back from Florida so quickly? I wondered who had contacted them, and then I thought what a horrible phone call that must have been to receive. I felt even more guilt.

I honestly don't know how they did it. Between all eleven of us, there always seemed to be something going on. Over the course of their relationship, they had run the gamut when it came to us kids. There have been multiple car accidents, hit and runs, shoplifting, drug abuse, alcoholism, suicide attempts, mental anguish, threats, dangerous and illegal parties, failing school, unplanned pregnancies, to name a few. I heard them say once, if it's not life threatening, we are not going to stress over it, and who could blame them? With that much going on, they had to pick their battles.

My suicide attempt was a big one.

This broke my mother. She was so upset, but even more than that, she was afraid. I have always been close to my mom. Even as an adult, when things go bad, I want my mommy. When I discuss this with her now, she still feels badly because she didn't know the depths of my depression. I hid it very well and made a point to never cause trouble or give her a reason to worry. I didn't want to hurt her so I wanted her to think everything was fine. So much of this came as a surprise to her, and it hurt her deeply.

I honestly do not remember anything that we may have spoken about. I think she was at a loss for words, so we just stayed there together, following the advice of the doctors that came in and out. How do two people who love each other talk about something like that, especially at first? How does that conversation begin? We couldn't really figure it out.

The doctors advised that once I checked out of the ER, I should go to another hospital for evaluation and help. My mother agreed as I'm sure she wasn't comfortable with me coming home after something as big as this. She wanted to do all she could to get me help. John was there for support, mainly for my mother. My father never came to visit, even when he found out, once again earning his reputation. I had other visitors, mostly family, including my sister Kelly's then boyfriend, later husband, Matt, who has always been very protective of me. He showed me nothing but support during this ordeal and many more to come, including the night of Clint's death. Looking back, I also wondered how they had told Kevin, my therapist. Last I had seen him, I had stormed out. Hearing that I had done this must have affected him. I would never find out how.

Cal didn't know what happened. I never discussed it with him and he never asked, but I know that he knew.

All of these people in my life were observing me, wondering what had happened and why. As for me, I simply felt...relief.

I had wanted help. That was why. Now I was going to get it. That being said, I wasn't thrilled with how it was going to go down. I was discharged after two days and checked into another hospital. This one I would be staying at for a little while. They instantly went through my belongings and anything sharp or with a long cord was taken out. I was then taken to my room and told the rules. The door was to stay open at all times. There was no phone in the room. No other patient was allowed in the room. I had a 9 p.m. bedtime and there was an on-sight tutor, so school was still going to happen.

This wasn't going to be easy.

The first couple of days I just wanted out. I remember using the phone by the front office a lot. I cannot remember who I called, but I do remember crying a lot and begging to go home. I was always denied.

The only thing I did like about my floor at the hospital was the other people, mainly because they were extremely interesting or funny or both. They also served as a warning to me. We all congregated in the common area. We sat and watched whatever someone had chosen to put on the television, but many times, I found myself watching the people coming and going even more.

There was a man who was an amazing violinist. He would skip

down the halls inviting all of us to come to his concert. Apparently it was in his room, but per the rules, we were not allowed in, so unfortunately there would be no audience for him. I soon realized how thankful I was for this rule. One time he came by where I was sitting with some friends. He had a magazine and was holding two different pages open with pictures on them. He showed them both to us and asked which picture we liked better. One was of a mountain and the other of a man's naked butt. He skipped away leaving us with a blank stare on our faces.

There was a woman who I enjoyed talking to, who seemed pretty cool. I would see her one day and then she would disappear for a couple days and then reappear. Coincidentally, I had noticed a locked door that I rarely ever saw anyone go through. You had to have a code to open it. I was told that the serious problems were on the other side of the door, like some *One Flew over the Cuckoo's Nest* type stuff. When the woman reappeared one day, I had learned that she had visited the "other side" of that door for a bit. She showed me her arms. She had taken a hanger--I am not sure how she got her hands on one--and had beaten her arms repeatedly with it. Both arms were almost completely black and blue and swollen.

I remember thinking...*I need to get my shit figured out!*

I knew I needed help and honestly, I was even a little relieved to be in a place where I could supposedly get it. So I eventually decided to settle in. As the days went by, I became more and more comfortable. I felt so safe there, and I needed the structure. I didn't mind the rules or the tasks. We were rewarded upon finishing them with a pizza night or movie night.

The big daddy of them all was getting to leave the hospital on an outing. This sounded great...until I found out we would be driving in a specially marked hospital van. I really didn't want this to happen. What if someone I knew saw me coming out of this hospital van? I panicked, but then I thought the chances of that happening in the middle of the week were slim. Right? Well, are you familiar with Murphy's Law? Sure enough, when we got to the movie theater for an outing, a family friend saw me come out of the van, and I was mortified. I was also pissed because I knew it was going to happen. I just knew.

The hospital did also provide me with some friendships that ran deep. After all, we all shared something in common. We were all at least a little damaged, and we had our experiences to tie us together. You get to know people pretty well when you are stuck with each other. There were two boys that were slightly younger than me. They were actually pretty funny, and they always got me laughing, which I needed. I really enjoyed their company, and we became friends...even after I found out later that it was their job to entice me to eat. The boys and I were like the three musketeers. We had class time together with our tutor, who looked like a movie star. We also had group therapy sessions. During one session, the homework was to bring in a song that symbolized how you felt. I assume someone must have heard me playing this song over and over in my room and decided to have a session around it. My song was "Change" by John Waite from the movie *Vision Quest*. The boys were scrambling around looking for music for themselves, so they asked me as I was the Soundtrack Queen. I told them no problem and handed them my *Flashdance* soundtrack. It made for quite an amusing therapy session.

With the structure, the safety, and the friendships I had developed, I actually grew quite attached to that place, which made it difficult when I was told I was going home. That was a scary notion. I had so many questions. Does everything just go back to normal now? Was I better? What about the voices in my head? What about these friendships, especially with the boys...is it just over now? Ironically enough, I ran into one of those boys outside of the hospital a little while later, at my school, no less, where he was starting as a freshman. He was sweet and we chatted, but something was definitely different. We were different on the outside. That's what I pondered most. What happens next?

And perhaps most important to a teenager, what are they saying about me at school?

When I initially swallowed the pills and spent the next couple days at the first hospital, my friends became concerned because I wasn't answering the phone and nobody was telling them what was going on. They were especially worried when I didn't show up for school the next day. I even heard something about them having an argument in front of the principal's office about what had gone down that night.

Eventually, somehow, some of my friends found out and, like things do in high school, it spread, and soon, everybody knew. I did have some of my close friends, Amy and Renee, actually come visit me in the hospital. I remember feeling like I didn't know what to say, which was strange; I was never speechless around them. So we didn't really talk about it. We just chatted for a while about inconsequential stuff like a big trip a bunch of them were taking to Daytona Beach for spring break. At the end of their visit, Amy handed me a beautiful letter and a cassette tape she wanted me to listen to with the song "Just the Way You Are" by Billy Joel on it. I never forgot that.

On my first day back at school, I held out hope that maybe not everybody knew, or even if they did, things could just go back to normal. As I walked down the hallway to my first period class I noticed a big banner with signatures.

"There is a girl named Kori Keefer, and we'd really like to keep her."

It was very sweet, but the jig was up, and I knew the rest of my high school experience was going to be a challenge.

CHAPTER 12
STEPPING OUT OF THE BOX

It's perhaps a little strange to say this, but the whole experience around my suicide attempt and what followed might be one of the best things that could have happened to me. Of course, I don't mean the attempt itself. That was a desperate, rash, and perhaps even selfish act. There were better ways I could have handled it and I still feel guilty for how it hurt the people I loved.

No, what I'm talking about was the help it gave me afterward, as well as the clarity. I felt like I was truly *heard* for the first time in a while, perhaps my entire life. For so long I had put up such a façade, even in my most desperate times of need, that nobody had known. Now they did. Now I did. Now I understood just how troubled I was and how important it was for me to bring myself back and get a grasp on my life and my journey, wherever it was leading. The whole experience enabled me to come back to my center, to ground myself. The voices in my head seemed to be calm, at least for the time being, and that was a huge relief.

I mentioned earlier that this was a turning point. This experience would set the stage (literally) for what was going to happen next. If it hadn't happened, I don't know what I would have done with my life, or if I would have survived.

Being back in school was just awkward, and I knew that my first step on my new path was going to be about getting through the rest of my time there. I don't remember discussing what happened too much, but I knew that everyone knew and I could sometimes hear the whispers. It didn't bother me as much as it might have someone else, but it was still something to endure. I didn't know what or how things would change for me when I got home, but I knew things were going to be different now, and sure enough they were. I still tried my best in school, hung out with friends, and continued a relationship with my boyfriend at the time, Jamie. He was a sweet guy who stuck with me through all of this. I always had two sides of me, especially in high school, and Jamie represented the more innocent side. I didn't drink, smoke, or party around him. He was more of my better side, which sometimes led to a distance between us, one that could have expanded during my stint in the hospital. But he stood by me, despite his hurt feelings and confusion, writing me amazing letters and poems to help get me through. I never forgot those acts of kindness and it's one of the reasons we're still friends today.

School, friends, boyfriend...it all was fine, but often seemed a little forced. I needed to find new meaning and purpose. That's what a life-altering event will do, and I've experienced a few. It's amazing all the opportunities and paths that open up in front of you when that happens, good and bad. It's also interesting to see what path your instincts lead you down.

For me, I refocused on my one true love...dance. No more drinking or partying, no more drama, no more bullshit. Just dance. Everything else took a back seat. Although most of my friends were thinking about college, it couldn't have been further from my mind. In fact, in wasn't on my mind at all. This had nothing to do with not liking school. It just didn't resonate with me and I knew it wasn't in my future. Not if I was going to do what I wanted to do, and that had become very important to me.

When you live with a sense of presence and awareness, the signs of who, where, or what you should be are all around. You can hear, see, and feel them. Now, following them is another story. At the time I was unconscious to this way of thinking. I know better now. Still, I knew enough to know I had to follow a dream that was itching at the back of my mind, even if it seemed uncomfortable, scary, or out of reach.

Since my first time of stepping out of the box, I have realized how important this is. Doing something against your natural tendencies allows not only for growth and a sense of self but you also see what it means to feel alive. What is the worst thing that could happen? So I make a complete fool out of myself. If so, so be it. We need to be able to laugh at ourselves. Besides, trying is always better than wondering "what if," right? After this experience, I didn't really think too much about whatever my next move would be. I just went for it. Then after the initial "oh shit, I hope I did the right thing" question, I knew I would become comfortable with my choice and would work forward from there. If we wait too long to make a decision, fear of the unknown tends to take over and we talk ourselves out of it. If we just go for it, then we have no choice but to work through any obstacles, which are usually only in our head anyway. Sometimes if we sit on things for too long the universe—in its own magical way—will give us a gentle push towards the edge. Then we have no choice but to make a move.

That's why after high school, I was moving to Hollywood.

I had visited California twice. The first time Joanie, my friend and studio owner, took a few of us girls to visit both of her sisters Julie and Jeanne, who were dancers/choreographers in L.A. and had their own professional dance troupe with celebrity students like Cristina Applegate and Drew Barrymore. That was when I first got the bug. Then I went myself for a couple of weeks the summer before my senior year. I stayed with Julie, and I auditioned for *Videopolis* which was at Disneyland at the time. I didn't make it through the second cuts. But in any case, I knew that's where I was moving as soon as I could.

I was going to pursue a career in dance. Keep in mind I was not some lead company dancer. I was just a girl from Toledo who loved performing. But I was ready to chase the impossible. When I mentioned my idea to my mother, she was in a state of disbelief. It wasn't like me to step out of my comfort zone. I was still quiet and shy, and I think she was concerned about me being able to handle it. When she saw I was serious, she talked my sister Kelly into going with me. She was dating Matt so I know it wasn't easy for her, but she did it for me. Despite the fact that I had some friends and contacts out there, I'm sure they were still worried about my mental stability, and the idea of me being out there without any family didn't sit well.

It's good to be loved.

Within a month of my graduation, we loaded up the car and drove cross country to L.A. After four days of being on the road, I will never forget my first glimpse of what I imagined California to be. We were driving on the 10 freeway towards Santa Monica. We went through a tunnel and within seconds there it was: the beautiful ocean, sun gleaming down on the waves, the sandy beach, and the palm trees. Since I was a little girl I had dreamed of living somewhere that had palm trees. I could barely handle the excitement.

This was my next step. This was where everything had led me, and I was ready to stop searching for stability and comfort and love and go make my own. I was ready to move on, to start *my* life. What better place than in the City of Angels. I was ready, eager, and excited for the challenges.

There would be challenges.

CHAPTER 13
STRAIGHT UP

Do it, and then figure it out later.

That has kind of been a pattern for me my whole life, and it certainly applied to my move out west. My sister Kelly and I really had no plan or strategy beyond moving to L.A. and seeing what would happen. It seemed as good a strategy as any.

Kelly had visited some friends for spring break the year prior and had fallen in love with the L.A. suburb of Calabasas, so that's where we found a place. It was good for her (and in some ways for me) because that was where her friends lived. Although beautiful, it was far from the studios and where I needed to be for auditions.

And it was a *long* way from Toledo. The switch to Los Angeles was definitely a culture shock. It wasn't just the cost of living and the traffic. It was the way of life and the people, and I'm not even talking about working in the industry yet! I honestly have to say I never felt fully comfortable. I am sure it was just my own insecurities. I didn't think I was as *cool* as those people. Suddenly...the voices showed up again.

Perhaps moving to L.A. had been a bit of a drastic step for somebody who was just finally learning to be comfortable with herself.

Regardless, we settled in pretty quickly. It wasn't long before Kelly was hired at the Cheesecake Factory up the road. I had never had a job other than teaching at my dance studio. Still, I applied, and I am pretty sure I was hired by association. I soon learned a steady job serving cheesecake wasn't for me. I went to work every day with a nervous stomach. I dreaded the first customer because I knew that meant that more were coming. It was not about the tips for me. I would have been completely happy having one table in my section for my whole shift. I was in the walk-in refrigerator crying at least once a week. I could not believe how rude people could be! I mean, I'm sure it had nothing to do with me being a *horrible* waitress. Still, I did manage to hold that job for six months, just enough time to try every cheesecake on the menu...twice! I was eventually fired for going to an audition rather than a scheduled shift and I was fine with that, vowing I would never work in the restaurant industry ever again. Little did I know...

Speaking of auditioning, it was a lot harder than I thought it was going to be. And I thought it was going to be tough! The worst part was that I was still battling with feelings of self-worth. Auditioning for anything in the entertainment industry in Hollywood just pulls all those feelings of insecurity out and back up to the surface.

I kept trying, but every audition I went to, I just knew I wouldn't get it. I would check out the room and just by watching how everyone acted, I could pick out who was going to be kept. I was so envious of their confidence. I would sit in the back of the room to watch everyone talking and laughing and seemingly enjoying the moment, not a nervous care in the world. It was amazing. We would soon be called all together to learn the combination. I would stand in the way back where there was no opportunity to even learn the first step let alone the entire combination, so I was doomed from the beginning. They would then give us a little time to go over it before calling a few of us out at a time by numbers. I would stand next to dancers doing it to try to pick up what I could, knowing very well that was impossible. The smarter thing to do would have been to leave, save any humility that I may have had left. I guess I loved to be tortured.

No, that's not it. I still wanted this badly, even if I didn't know how to build the confidence to pursue it. Plus, I have never been one to quit on something important to me. So I would always stay, make a fool of myself, then grab my things and go home.

To further my frustration, I began to notice that it was the same dancers who were getting all the jobs. At least it seemed that way. I started to question the business itself (I wasn't the first or the last) as well as my own talent. I realized that through my frustration with wanting something but not knowing how to get it, the lack of confidence came through.

This was a whole other ball game than the studio in Toledo.

I did keep up with my training, taking class with the colleagues I knew out there as well as a few other studios. Eventually, I did get my first gig as a backup dancer in a movie called *Hollywood Chaos* with a little help from Jeanne. It was such a fun experience. I loved being in front of the camera; I loved rehearsing! I spent the next year taking dance classes and going to auditions, just trying to break in any way I could. There were some good moments... and then there were moments like my audition for *A Funny Thing Happened on the Way to the Forum*.

Most of the auditions I got through friends and colleagues, but this particular one was different. I got a message from someone I didn't know telling me about a musical audition. I hadn't ever auditioned for a musical, just TV or movies where I could let my legs do the performing. The person said I would need prepared music.

Meaning I had to sing.

Let me take a quick sidetrack here. I once was briefly cast in a group of four pretty dancers who were supposed to be a band... called I.B.Fine by the way. Seriously. We were supposed to sing "hip and cool" songs about not doing drugs. Yes, I'm aware of the irony.

We actually performed live lip synching to previously recorded tracks and focused on our choreography. Even when Julie, the choreographer who got us the gig dropped out, sensing this was a shady arrangement, we stuck with it, recording, rehearsing, doing photo shoots and more. This lasted for about six months before we showed up for rehearsal one day to see the studio completely cleaned out. We never got paid a dime. I wouldn't find out until much later that there had been a fight between producers, a gun had been pulled, and that was that. I.B.Fine was done, as was my music star career. Which was actually fine...because I couldn't really sing.

So yeah, back to the audition. I needed to prepare music. I didn't think too much of it, thinking I could just focus on the dance part and all would be well. So I chose a song that I thought I could do for a classic musical that would help me show my chops.

"Straight Up" by Paula Abdul.

The morning of the audition, I put on my cutest dance leotard, grabbed my music, negotiated the insane traffic leading into downtown L.A., got to the location and...

...the same group of dancers I always saw weren't there.

"This is cool, maybe I have a chance at this one."

Then I noticed that the few people who were there were only warming up their voices and not their bodies.

Uh oh.

I sat next to this girl giving off the most easy-going vibe and asked her about her music. She actually had a huge binder of music that she was looking through. To give myself a little comfort, I asked if she was a good singer. "Not really," she replied and I was comforted in the fact that I wasn't alone.

Soon after, they called us all up to learn the dance combination we would be performing for them. It was very easy and very obvious I could dance, so I was kept. I was on cloud nine. Then one by one they were calling people in to give their music to the pianist. There was no special order, so I kept going to the end of the line. I eventually stood behind the girl who "couldn't really sing." As the door closed behind her, I put my ear up to it.

Holy shit!

She sounded like a fricking angel! Apparently we had different ideas of what not being able to sing was; when I say I cannot do something, I mean I cannot do it.

Fight or flight instinct took over as I realized this was my last chance. I walked out, stopped, thought for a minute, and said, "Fuck it!" I turned around and walked in, straight up to the pianist, and handed him my music. There were three other people, who I'm assuming were the director, choreographer, and casting director. What happened next I really wanted to put out of my head, and have done so for quite a while but...

Put it this way, I would have made the worst audition at *American Idol* sound good. In the music that I gave him, there were the backup parts. I was singing Paula's lines, but my nerves took control and I ended up singing all three parts, barely managing to fit all the words in because well, *it's not possible!* God bless them, they let me finish the entire song. Now, of course I realize why...I am pretty sure I was the comic relief that gave them a laughable end to their very long day.

That audition pretty much summed up my early auditioning years in L.A. Still, I was managing to survive. I was stubborn enough to find a way. I had a few friends, the occasional date, and a purpose, which was the main thing I needed. That purpose kept me alive. Now I just needed some more regular work to help me not only afford to live in L.A., but to boost a pretty beaten down self-confidence.

I eventually found it in my next great adventure on a cruise ship... that should have *never* been allowed to leave port. In more ways than one, however, that cruise ship would show me the world.

CHAPTER 14
YOUNG AND NAIVE

Ok, so the cruise ship itself didn't show me the world. In fact, it only showed me a small portion of the Pacific Ocean between San Diego and Ensenada, Mexico.

Every. Single. Day.

Perhaps you're thinking that life on a cruise ship is glamorous. I know I did. Well, it's not. Especially when it's a foreign ferry converted into a cruise ship and run by Greeks who weren't overly concerned with regulations and/or safety. The ship was very top heavy and had absolutely no stabilizers, which means even the slightest waves rocked the boat back and forth. The part of the ocean we traveled seemed to always

have high swells, and the dancers often ended up either in the band stand or the audience, depending upon which way the ship was rocking. The ship had been refurbished in pieces and had a good face on it, but if you looked closely, there were problems everywhere, so much so it seemed like the ship was barely hanging on. The captain and crew didn't speak English, and the ship was *loaded* with booze, not necessarily just for the travelers. It was a big party, and it was clear that was the top priority.

As if that wasn't enough, because there was a crew shortage, we dancers, myself included, were in charge of helping to lower the life boats in case of emergency, like the ship sinking. Yeah, I don't remember that being mentioned at the audition. The day the whole crew had the emergency drill, you would have thought we were shooting a *Three Stooges* episode. Yet, nobody on the ship really seemed too concerned with our performance, or attempt, I should say. How the Coast Guard ever allowed us to leave the port was beyond me.

But I was dancing and getting paid $300 a week to do so. I was ecstatic! I also made some good friends on that ship, including the other dancers and singers that had been cast with me and my choreographer. The ship itself, despite all its issues, was like a playground for us. The band was absolutely amazing and gave the dancers all the energy we needed. We used to sit and just listen to them play for hours. And partying wasn't a problem. It didn't seem like there was anybody there to monitor our behavior, and if there was, they didn't care. I was having the time of my life, far removed from the anger, frustration, depression, and more I had felt back in Toledo. I was leaving that part of me behind and was living in the present, wondering what my next great adventure would be.

Turns out, it would be a photographer from Wales. His name was Craig Jones, and he had the privilege of taking pictures of the guests during embarkation and debarkation. I will never forget the day Craig came aboard the ship. Imagine Hugh Grant in his twenties, both in appearance and voice. He was so cute, and I was attracted to him right away. He was very quiet and reserved, one to sit back and just take it all in. He kept you guessing, but was also very sweet. When he did open his mouth, the things that came out were hysterical; he had the driest sense of humor, especially when talking about tourists he met. The accent made it all the better. We dancers took him under our wing right away. We had been on the ship for a few weeks by the time he joined us, so we knew what there was to do for fun in Ensenada and in San Diego. I noticed that he spent a lot of time looking at me.

I would soon come to realize that he not only liked me, he liked me for me. I know that might not sound like a big deal, but it was. He was sweet, genuine, funny, handsome...and he liked me! He could also be very romantic. There was a song from the Yardbirds called "For Your Love" that he used to sing in my ear, even though he couldn't sing. Add the accent, and it used to make me laugh. He also had a riddle that he would tell me all the time. He would never give me the answer, hoping that one day I would figure it out. It used to make me crazy! I was in awe, fully realizing for the first time that this was what a relationship could be. We became a thing quite quickly...and as I've shown, when I go in on a relationship, I go all in.

Which made it harder when his visa expired a few months into our being together and he had to return to England.

We were heartbroken. The plan for me was to finish my three-month cruise contract and then go meet him in England. I had never been overseas, and honestly, hadn't really thought about it until then. I needed motivation to go explore, and Craig definitely gave me what I needed. We had discussed the possibility of me getting on a cruise ship over there by auditioning in England. I actually called and asked if they would even hire Americans. They didn't say no.

So I packed up all my things with my headshots and resume and headed over. Oh, the one thing I forgot to bring with me (because I didn't have one) was a work visa. Apparently they frown upon that in other countries just as much as they do here. I was so young and naïve. I spoke with Craig on the phone right before I took off from the airport, just so thrilled to be going on this new adventure! I spent the entire flight eager with the anticipation of seeing him and starting the next adventure.

I almost didn't make it out of the London airport.

As I passed through customs, the official took my passport. He was just about ready to stamp it when he asked me why I was there, and if I would try to get work. When I said yes, they told me to come with them. The customs officer walked me over to this woman who was not very welcoming. She took one look at me, told me I was in trouble, and threatened that I might be sent home. She grabbed my luggage and carry-on bag, walked me to a room, and left me there. Apparently they announced my name over the loudspeaker and told whoever was there to meet me to come to this office. Poor Craig had driven a couple hours to pick me up. We only had known each other a couple months so he was a bit nervous as to what the problem could be. And I'm sure he was questioning this decision. I know I was. They held me for three very long hours. Finally they brought me to a room where they had been going through all of my things, including the portfolio of pictures. They then proceeded to tell me that it was actually legal for me to get a job on a cruise ship because it would be in international waters and not on British soil. They gave me my things and walked me to where Craig was nervously waiting to see what the outcome would be.

Saying I was happy to see him would be an understatement.

Thus began my international adventures. He showed me all around London, all the touristy stuff, and then we headed to North Wales where his family lived. His family home was actually the old toll house to a bridge in Rhyl, a beautiful and charming seaside resort town.

His parents, as well as his younger brother and sister, welcomed me in with open arms. Everyone in his family was very close, and they all seemed to love each other. I ended up staying with them in Wales for a month, at which point my visa was up. All I had to do was leave the country and come back and that would renew it for another month. Craig and I decided to take advantage of it and backpack around Europe, eventually making our way to Israel.

Why Israel? Well, the idea was to hopefully find work on a kibbutz, an agricultural commune. Craig's sister had done it and said the experience was rewarding, so we thought it would be a great adventure. Normally you apply to some company and they help you locate and apply to the kibbutz, setting you up. Instead, we decided to wing it.

Again, young and naïve.

Also, unprepared. I was still pretty shy and very easily intimidated. I think I was a little overwhelmed with what we were about to embark upon. I never think about the details. The concept was great, but I didn't realize all the work that would go into it as well. We never had a clear plan of where we were going or staying, which was difficult for me because I liked the idea of security. We had our backpacks that were too heavy and sleeping bags that were too thin, which is not very smart when we were planning on sleeping outdoors in March.

On the way, we traveled on a Eurorail pass. We stopped in Paris, Barcelona, Innsbruck, Bern, Rome, Athens, and the islands of Cypress and Corfu. We were on a tight budget, so we camped out most places. As incredible as it was seeing all the sites, I was miserable most of the time because I hate being cold... and it was cold!

By the time we were headed to Israel, which was a three-day boat ride from Greece, we were pretty much broke. We had just enough money to buy the tickets. I was so excited by the thought of a cabin with a bunk bed and possibly even a shower. Unfortunately, all we could afford were tickets for transportation only, and not a cabin. I was already starting to feel sick, and this wasn't going to help. We nestled into a warm corner of the ship outside the bridge, where we were shaded from the wind, and just held on. It was a long three days.

We arrived in Tel Aviv and after some sightseeing; we hopped on a bus that would take us about three hours outside of the city to a kibbutz in Ein Gedi, Israel. We were dropped off at the end of a long dirt road and began the trek up to the entrance. The whole time our fingers were crossed, hoping they would take us in. If they didn't, we didn't know what we were going to do. That's the problem with winging it. After some questions and a couple phone calls, the owner took us in. Lucky for us!

The rules were simple. They would put us up and feed us. We would work six days a week at the resort located on the coast of the Dead Sea, with Sundays off. For every week worked, we earned a half day. That way we could build up days to travel to other places. We were thinking Egypt. Craig's job was to serve food at the spa. I had to clean guest houses, which was worse than it sounds. The spa was a popular place for people trying to treat skin conditions...so the rooms were often awful. You can imagine. Oh, and the pay was $1.69 a day. All the volunteers were housed on what was named "The Moon" because it was the highest point of the kibbutz. There were about twenty-five of us, and I was the only American, so I was the "bloody yank" of the group. In the evening when everyone was done working, it became one big party. The beer tabs of the volunteers were long and no one had the money to pay them off.

Honestly, I could write a whole other book about this experience...the work, the personalities, the nights, the time with Craig.

We spent about a month working and then I became very home-sick. We asked if we could leave a couple days short of the time we said we would stay, and the man who brought us in was pretty angry. I really believe they were hoping to get more time out of us because we actually did our jobs up to their standard. We were asked to leave that night.

After a long drive back to Tel Aviv, an argument over money with a cab driver, and an uncomfortable stay in an overpriced hotel, I was anxious just to get home. Unfortunately, both our credit cards were declined when trying to purchase flights. I had to call home. Thankfully my mom was just as excited for me to get back as I was. We made our way back to Wales and soon after, I flew home.

And when I say home, I mean Toledo. Because of my adventures, both on the cruise and overseas, I no longer had my L.A. apartment anymore. Honestly, by that point, I didn't have my L.A. *life* anymore!

What I did have was a little more life experience, a guy I was crazy about, and a new perspective on things...which all served to set me up for the next grand adventure, more turmoil, and eventually to what I thought might have been my salvation.

CHAPTER 15
FAKE IT
TIL YOU MAKE IT

A short time after I got home to Toledo, I realized it wasn't where I wanted to be. I was instantly unhappy. It was mainly because, after just two years, I was no longer following my original plan, one that wasn't going to happen as long as I was in Ohio. I was stuck in the place I couldn't get away from fast enough after graduation.

I went back to teaching at the dance studio. It was definitely a strange feeling going back after such high hopes of accomplishing a set of goals that didn't seem overly ambitious to me. I had a little success, but not nearly enough to qualify for making my dream come true. I seemed to be picking up the pieces of my old life and building on that once again, which bothered me.

Luckily Craig was on his way, and all would be great, or so I thought. I had very strong feelings for him at this point, especially after all of our adventures together, and he was someone who made me very happy. After a few months, he met me in Toledo, moving into the basement (which was actually like a small apartment). A pretty easy-going guy, Craig was happy with this set up and with being near me. My entire family fell in love with him, although I know my stepfather never understood a word he said--Craig's accent threw John off big time. He would just look at Craig, smile and laugh, and then turn to me and ask, "What did he just say?" All seemed well.

But it wasn't.

As time went on, I began to slip more and more into my sadness. I questioned what I was doing with my life. I felt like I had totally failed, and I was so unhappy with myself. This began to take a toll on our relationship. Craig was so sweet, caring, and loving. But that wasn't enough. I soon realized I couldn't stay in Toledo. And even though I knew he was a great thing for me, I think I realized that I couldn't stay with Craig. It just wasn't part of the plan, and the longer I stayed in Toledo, the more important the plan became.

His six-month visa eventually ran out, and he had to return home. We left things very up in the air as neither of us seemed to know what we wanted. No, that's not true. Craig knew what he wanted, but it wasn't meshing with the dream that was constantly calling me. It hurt because I did care so deeply for him, and I will never forget the horrible pain of saying goodbye to him. Even though nothing was settled at that point, I think I knew that was it.

With Craig gone, and with him the last thing that was keeping me in Toledo, the only question was what to do next.

Move to Las Vegas, of course.

The idea of moving to Vegas was planted about a year prior when I met a singer during the shooting of a film I was in, *Hollywood Chaos*. She said there were a lot of jobs in Vegas for dancers and singers, not only in the hotels but in traveling shows as well. As I was contemplating a move, I knew I didn't want to go back to L.A. There were too many dancers and not enough opportunities and I just felt like that part of my life was over. I had never been to Vegas; I heard it was thrilling; and I knew absolutely no one.

It sounded perfect.

So I loaded up the car and made the trip cross country for the second time. As soon as I arrived, I rented an apartment...if you could even call it that. You could rent them by the week. The apartment reminded me of a hospital room; it was a studio apartment with a TV propped up in the corner. It was incredibly small, and I remember not feeling at home and almost a little afraid to even leave. Some very interesting characters were hanging around. In my short time there, I would peek out the window and see shady people doing shady things that I thought would be better to ignore. I remember hearing that they had actually found a dead body in the back of the complex. It was not the best place I've ever lived. Still, it was a place in a new city full of potential.

Poor Craig. Not long after he left, I stopped calling and writing. I totally broke off all contact. I didn't do this to hurt him or even to protect me. It was just that...as soon as he was going, my dream to get back into a dance career became the *only* thing of importance. It was a weight I carried with me and I didn't have room for anything else. We had plans to reconnect after I got settled, but I lost touch with him, despite all the times and different ways he tried to reach me.

It's not something I'm proud of.

I was in Vegas for just three days before I got my first audition for Siegfried and Roy's stage show. I was told to show up in between their performances for them to audition me. Just like my *Forum* audition, I really don't know what I was thinking. I had definitely been out of practice. I had gained a few extra pounds from my European travel where the least expensive food was bread and cheese. I also showed up wearing a black leotard and black nylons because I couldn't find my dance tights.

Great first impression.

They brought me to this corridor backstage where they taught me a dance combination. I was so nervous, I couldn't focus at all. They then took me out on the huge stage. A lot was going on.

The backstage crew was pre-setting for the next show, the waitresses were cleaning off the tables, the techs in the light booth were working with the lighting, the sound guys were working on the sound so the music was fluctuating from soft to booming through the speakers. There I was standing in the middle of all this commotion as they started my music. Before I knew it, I had already missed my cue. They stopped the music and started it again. The second time around was no better. There was no point in a third time.

Luckily not all was lost. I had found out that there was a dancer in the show looking for a roommate. When I went for the interview, I fell in love with her house. It was in the beautiful community of Summerlin, about twenty minutes north of the Las Vegas strip. It was so plush and green, you would never believe it was in the middle of the desert. The house had a pool and a beautiful backyard with flowers and palm trees. It was truly a little oasis. She asked if I could move in the following week. I asked if there was any way I could move that up seven days. I just couldn't stay another minute in that bizarre apartment building. Luckily, she agreed.

Toni, my new roommate, was great. She had been dancing for Siegfried and Roy for a few years. As we got closer, she would invite me to the cast parties. I loved meeting and hanging out with the dancers. I wanted so much to be dancing in any of the hotel shows. The more and more I met and spent time with these other dancers, I began to notice some special qualities they had and what I was lacking.

I finally realized that I was working against myself. I was my biggest road block. Every time I walked into an audition, I had the attitude that everyone else was better than me. From the moment I walked in and looked around, I was sending that energy out. The results I expected and set myself up for happened each and every time. I made a deal with myself. Beginning with the next audition, I was going to walk in like I owned the place. I was going to place myself front and center where I would be noticed, rather than in the back, hiding in the crowd. I was going to commit. I was going to exude confidence, whether I felt it or not. I was going to sell it! No more insecurity bullshit. It was time for me to pick up my head and stop being such a wimp.

That's when I developed my mantra: "Fake it 'til you make it!"

I walked into any audition ready to work, like I had been there a million times. I would smile and laugh and talk to the other dancers like I could care less about being nervous. Sure enough, once my total outward attitude changed, the confidence was noticed. Bam, it worked! And soon, I actually *became* what I was putting out there. I was less intimidated in Vegas. I worked hard and was dedicated and motivated to not give up. There were a lot of cool shows in Vegas at the time. There were awesome and intense choreographers that I had the chance to work with, and I was not going to miss out.

After a month or so of auditioning, I was brought in for a show called *Pizzazz* with acclaimed choreographer Michael Darrin (most notably known for directing Paula Abdul's "Cold-Hearted Snake" video and some Academy Awards programs, along with stage shows). It was actually outside of Vegas in Wendover, but it was a three-month engagement to dance!

Now, at any audition I would attend, I would put my game face on. I felt really good and I committed to exuding as much confidence as I could to be like those other dancers. The audition was at a place I had actually been to before. I had done well at this past audition, and I was held until the end. Unfortunately they lined me up next to the other dancers, and I was cut because I was three inches taller.

Not this time.

I walked in and joined the other dancers who were quietly warming up and putting on their shoes. I stayed focused and present, not looking around at the other dancers. There were two long tables at the front where the producer, choreographer, assistant choreographer, and a couple others were sitting facing us. We were told to bring our pictures and resumes up to them and then spread out to learn the choreography. I positioned myself front and center and smiled at all of them. I noticed they were looking over the photos and pointing and talking as we all arranged ourselves in view of the choreographer. I had tunnel vision as I learned the combination. We all learned it count by count. Then they put the music on and we practiced a couple times through. They had us switch lines so the people in the back could now move to the front, and we practiced it again. They told us all to sit down and then called ten of us up by name and arranged us to match our pictures on the table in front of them.

I felt good about the combination. My confidence was high the only thing I needed to do now was sell it! I pretended like it was just a dance class, so there was no reason to be nervous. The music started and I was off. Before I realized, it was done. We switched lines and did it one more time. As I went to the back to sit down and let the other group come up, I couldn't help but notice the excitement rise in me. I knew I did well.

Sure enough, I booked it and soon, I was dancing!

That was only the beginning...

CHAPTER 16
DO YOU
REMEMBER ME?

As my career got rolling, I was always checking the "Dirt Alert," which was a listing of audition notices in Vegas, a much easier and more accessible system than what I experienced in L.A. One day I noticed an audition for a television show in Milan, Italy. The show was called *Il Grande Circo*.

Italy! It was all I could think about. What an amazing adventure it would be to be dancing there. I *was* going to land this part, no matter what.

I had been going to the gym, and I had lost my bread and cheese weight so I was feeling pretty good. I went to the audition and did exactly what I had promised myself I would do. I placed myself in the front, acting very confident. I was totally faking it of course, but when all was said and done, I felt great...and guess who was on her way to Milan!

I could hardly believe it. I was just twenty-one years old and now I was going to be dancing professionally on screen in Italy.

In less than a year, I had gone from feeling like I had missed my opportunity or was at least so far behind in the pursuit of my dream that I wouldn't be able to recover to being what I felt was light years ahead. It was all so thrilling!

There were twenty American dancers hired for the show. They would pay for our flights and put us up. We would also be getting a little living per diem. When we arrived, they picked us up and took us to the apartments where we would be staying until we had our permanent place which was closer to the city. All the actors--who were well-known in Italy--had already been hired for the show. There were some challenges of course, beyond the heavy work and rehearsal schedule. Mainly, there was quite the language barrier, especially at rehearsals. The choreographer didn't speak English, and the assistant only spoke a little. It probably added twice as much time to rehearsals and filming. Still, we were living in Italy, dancing, and soaking up the culture and this tremendous opportunity.

Then there was the producer.

He was the one who had hired us, and he was with us for the first few weeks. He would go back and forth from the US to Italy, and we enjoyed ourselves a lot more when he was away. He could be a little crazy, to say the least. An American, he was a small man, shorter than five feet tall, with a high-pitched voice. He was loud, boisterous, erratic, moody, sensitive, and sometimes, just plain mean. Eventually we saw a pattern with his mood swings. He would be so sweet at times, then it was like someone flipped a switch. When this happened, you did not want to be in his line of fire. When he was in a good mood, he seemed to have a lot of energy and he talked a lot. We all had our suspicions as to what caused his highs and his lows.

There was one thing he said to us that I will never forget, something that essentially defined him. I still laugh about it today. We were all in the dressing room, putting on our makeup and getting ready. He came busting through the dressing room door, and we all fell silent. By this point we were so used to his mood swings, that it was always interesting to see which way he was going to go. He took one look at all of us and said, "Girls, girls...ignore your facial features and paint a pretty picture!" Without hesitating, he turned around, walked out, and slammed the door behind him. We all had to stop ourselves from laughing out loud.

Unfortunately, he meant every word he said, and I was starting to get a good glimpse of what this business was really all about. Professional dancing was not a good choice of careers for someone who lacked self-esteem, and producers like him certainly didn't help. You had to have a tough shell. I was not sure I fit in that category. One day I was running down to catch the bus that we took every day to the studios. He stopped me before I got on and asked where my roommate was. I told him she was in the shower but she would be on her way down soon. He was in a foul mood that day. He looked right at me and said, "I hope she is washing the fat off of her!" I took this personally as I've always been sensitive to people dealing with weight issues. I sometimes became his target. What can I say? We were in Italy, and the craft service table was always carb loaded.

There was also an Italian producer for the show, and he too was a character in his own right. From what I gathered, he was pretty big time, a late forties Italian who was funny but serious in his business and, like many of the Italian men we met, very aggressive. Still, for the most part, he liked me. In fact, one night he asked me out, and we had a fun time--

Wait.

No.

No, we didn't.

I promised to be honest. As much as I'd like to say it was just a gay old innocent time, it wasn't. He crossed a line, despite my telling him not to expect anything from me and his promises that he wouldn't try anything physical with me. At the time, it made me angry, but I blew it off. I would learn over the course of my career, through many encounters and conversations with other dancers, that this was simply part of the business. I would see it time and time again. I honestly didn't think much of it until more recently, and now it makes my skin crawl. Perhaps it's because I'm older and have more perspective. Perhaps it's because I'm so far removed from the industry. Or perhaps it's because I have daughters of my own. Regardless, thinking about it now infuriates me. That "date" wasn't even close to the worst thing I experienced in this regard. I had actually experienced much worse earlier on in my life, thanks partially to a silver-tongued older man who knew how to prey on the innocent, and mainly to my own naïveté.

OK, so I'm realizing I have to take another time out. I haven't gotten to everything quite yet. The things that I have come clean on up to now have been difficult to get out, mainly because I am so ashamed and embarrassed by my actions...or sometimes, the lack thereof. The reason I don't like being classified as a victim is because I don't like giving up that power. But in this case, and in a couple others in my life, I *was* a victim because I was unaware. I was trusting and unsure how certain situations were supposed to be handled. That lack of awareness sometimes got me into trouble, and this was one of the worst. I had skipped this story initially, but I realize that it is part of my life story. If I'm following my own rules with this book, I need to get it out there.

For me and for any young woman who finds herself in this position.

When I was younger, before I headed to California, I went to see a photographer about getting headshots done. I was very excited as it seemed like a big step in preparing for my career. I could barely contain my excitement as I picked out my most flattering outfits. He seemed like a nice man, and I met him at his home. We talked through what I was looking for, and he gave me some suggestions. I just wanted to have a few different photos that would work at different auditions. He brought me downstairs to a room in his basement that was set up like a studio. There was a futon in the room which was a little weird, but who was I to judge? I was just getting into this business and really knew nothing of how it worked.

I think I felt a little off when he was showing me these sexy pictures of beautiful women that apparently he had taken. He said he was trying to get a feel for what I wanted, but it made me uncomfortable. In some, the women were nude, but it was tastefully done. I wasn't sure why he was showing them to me. I think now he was maybe testing the waters.

Yes, I would soon learn that's exactly what he was doing.

I'll never forget that there was a little girl in her jammies upstairs playing and watching cartoons in the living room when I had first came in. She was just sweetly playing by herself. It actually brought me comfort. I thought, "Ok, this is a safe situation, what could happen?"

Exactly what you think happened, and I still struggle to this day with whose fault it was, really. First of all, I had just turned eighteen. Though I was still young, I now looked at myself as an adult. I should have known better. But I was also still sweetly innocent and trusting, which is exactly what a predator looks for in his prey.

I honestly am not sure how it progressed from looking at pictures of models in magazines to me posing nude. I had a leather jacket, and I don't know exactly what he said, but he mentioned wearing the jacket with nothing under but without showing anything. I actually didn't mind that, that seemed cool. Then he asked me to take my clothes off, and he started guiding me in what to do. Why was I listening to him? Why didn't I do anything? Probably because that wasn't me. I wasn't there. It was the first time in my life that I actually shut down and left my body. That's the only way it could have happened. I was just as disgusted watching this stupid girl with no backbone as she did what he said. None of it felt right, but how do you stop once you have gone that far? Literally the next thing I remember, I was naked, letting him shoot very distasteful photos of me.

Then it was done. I cannot remember how long this went on or how we wrapped up. I don't even remember gathering my things and walking myself upstairs. What I do remember is looking at the little girl playing in the living room as I walked out. I was so mad at her. She was the reason I felt safe. It was all her fault.

It's taken me a while to really process this. The photographer was horrible. No, he did not force me, but he certainly manipulated me. I believe he prayed on my weakness and that is where my anger comes from. He knew this was wrong. I knew it was wrong too. It was just another situation with men where I went against everything inside of me to avoid disappointing them, and I paid the price. I swallowed this down for years and never told a soul. In fact, I tried hard to not think about that day, to bury it far down into the recesses of my brain. I would try not to think of him, but I would see his face through my eyes, with his little fucking camera.

A couple years later, when I was back home visiting from California, I was leaving a restaurant and as I walked out I noticed this man walking toward me. It was like the hairs on my arms stood straight up. It was him. As he walked by me, he dropped his keys. I watched him pick them up off the ground. The blood began to boil inside of me. Every part of me wanted to look him in the face and tell him what I thought of him and how that experience had haunted me.

"Do you remember me, you disgusting pig? Was that your little girl upstairs playing that day? What did you do with those pictures anyway? Do you have any remorse for what you did, or am I one of many? How could you do this?"

Instead, with a sick feeling in my gut, I quietly walked to the car, got in, and drove away.

I have still not dealt with this particularly horrible experience and the shame I feel about it. I'm not sure I'll ever know how to rid myself of it completely, and maybe I'm not supposed to so I can help make sure others don't find themselves where I was.

Which leads me back to my "date" with the producer in Italy. As the producer, he hung around on set quite a bit and we befriended him. When he eventually asked me out, I found myself in a bit of a slippery situation. I didn't really want to go because I wasn't into him and I didn't want him to get the wrong idea, but I was afraid of saying no and getting on his bad side. So I agreed, begrudgingly.

He took me to a comedy club and out to dinner. After dinner he went to great lengths to get me to come to his hotel room. He promised he would not try anything on me. In fact, his actual words were, "Just come up to my room with me and let me prove to you that you can trust me." He said he just wanted to have a glass of wine with me. I believed him and said ok.

I know, I know.

We left and went to where he was staying. And then, believe it or not, the hotel concierge wouldn't let me in because they thought I was a prostitute! A big argument occurred––I don't speak Italian so I didn't know what was happening. We got in a cab where he continued to tell me we were going to the police station so they could give proof that I was there on a working visa and I was not a prostitute.

All of this for a glass of wine?

He finally was able to prove this, and we went back to the hotel. After a bit more arguing, we went up to his room. We were there for less than a minute and he was all over me. I was furious.

"You promised! I told you I didn't want this!"

He tried to coerce me, certain he was going to break me down. He even got me on the bed, but I was stiff as a board...legs, arms, nothing was going to be pried open. As angry as I was, I was never afraid. I felt like he would only take this so far and, I don't know, maybe I was a little wiser, stronger, and more experienced. Maybe I felt like I could handle this, regardless of how much I had misread the situation once again. I was pissed, but in control. He ended up getting mad, and I said I was going to leave.

"Fine, go," he said. "But if you do leave, then I am a liar and you are a prostitute."

He had a point and I don't know why, but it bothered me. I couldn't have them thinking that about me, so I didn't leave. I stayed, completely dressed, lying on the edge of the bed, waiting for the sun to come up.

While there are some similarities in these two stories, especially in the naïveté that led me to these situations, there are also some major differences. I'm just realizing this now, but one I let happen and one I didn't. These two instances taught me a lot about the ugly side of the business and well, people in positions of power in general. More than that, they taught me about control. I started out writing this chapter to talk about my Italy experience, and it's become something else. I guess that is the point of writing; to get it out there. I was disgusted in every way by what happened to me in the basement of that photographer's house, but as I write it down and compare it to what *could* have happened with my producer in Italy, I see not just a major difference, but also a major shift in who I was and what I was becoming. In that sense, in that one way, as I was about to get lost in the other traps and dark corners of this challenging industry, I could keep some power, some control. Perhaps, even though it was subconscious, knowing I had that little bit of control in me was the spark that would eventually pull me out of those dark places.

I would be visiting those places very soon.

CHAPTER 17
DO IT FULL OUT!

For as exciting as my time in Italy was, I started to grow tired, not just with the work, but the experience as a whole and even some of the people involved. The experience with my producer had put me off with him and the production as a whole. Don't get me wrong, I still loved what I was doing, and I was thrilled to meet so many prestigious and talented people in Italy, as well as a whole big group of new friends. I also loved the country, seeing all the sites and the clubs and parties. It was a whirlwind experience that was perfect for a young artist in her early twenties. But I started to miss some of the comforts of home and a sense of normalcy in my life. I actually started putting some of the weight back on which prompted the American producer to start calling me fat as well. This culminated in a live New Year's Eve show that I could barely get through without crying.

I also missed Craig, and I started to realize exactly what I had done to him. The guilt completely consumed me. We had loved each other and were building something, and then I had just dropped him. It wasn't so much that my dreams had become so important. That happens. Priorities shift. But the fact that I just abandoned him completely was absolutely awful. Now, as the whirlwind was slowing down, all I had done to him was coming to the surface, and I was devastated.

After debating with myself back and forth, I got a hold of him one day. He was so upset but remained calm.

"You just disappeared...I thought you were dead."

That was when it really sunk in. I was a wreck. I begged him to come to Italy, and he actually agreed. I was so happy and wondered if there was a way we could pick up the pieces. Or perhaps find a way to balance our lives and careers with a relationship.

But Craig didn't come to see me to start anew. He came to say goodbye.

He came to visit for a couple days as that was all he could spare. Though we had a good time, and it felt so good to be with him, I realized this pretty quickly. Even before he left, I sunk deeper into sadness as the reality of everything, of what I had done, set in. As he departed, he embraced me with a sad but loving hug. We were saying goodbye at the airport, and I was crying. He leaned over and whispered the answer to our little riddle. Then he gave me another hug and off he went.

Thus ended the Craig relationship, this time for good.

I was ready to head back to the States and to do a show on stage where I could perform a whole number without having to "cut" and start over a million times. When we finished with the live show on New Year's, half of us headed back to the US. The other half had met significant others and decided to stay for a while. I couldn't wait to get back to see what my next move would be.

I got back to work in Vegas, auditioning and waiting to see where my career would take me next. Soon enough came another Michael Darrin show. It would be at a beautiful five-star theater in Branson, Missouri. I wasn't that excited about the temporary move to Branson, but it was a brand new show, so I would get to be there from the very beginning. Plus, I really wanted to work with Michael again.

I should talk for a minute about Michael as he was, in many ways, one of the most influential people in my life, especially in regards to my dance career. He was someone that showed me that I did in fact have a lot of strength...and that I liked to be pushed to my limits.

We began rehearsals for the show in Vegas. Michael was finishing up somewhere else so he joined us after three weeks. When he returned, he came in to watch us perform what we had learned so far.

That was not a good day for us.

Michael was a master choreographer. He was well-respected in the industry and was truly a genius. He also had a reputation for being extremely intense, to the point of terrifying. He tolerated nothing but the very best and would let you know if you weren't living up to his standards.

From the moment he returned, rehearsals were no more games. I was so scared of him. Nothing was ever good enough. His choreography was awesome and beautiful, but he also loved using props in his numbers. So on top of learning the intricate choreography, we had to throw in props of all varieties. There was no room for error. Ever.

"I'm the choreographer! You are the fucking dancer! Do it full out!"

This threw so many dancers off. There were a lot of dancers who wouldn't work with him because he was so tough. But not me and not our cast. We pulled together as a team and worked through his aggressive, perfectionist style as a unit, supporting each other and pushing each other to meet his demands.

Honestly, I loved it.

I not only gained so much respect for him, I *understood* him. I desired that kind of greatness. I wanted to push myself to not only impress him, but to go beyond his standards. I had never worked so hard in my life and I was up for it! I was so much better because of him, and I did well with this kind of motivation. A compliment, or even a smile, was very uncommon. So when he did take notice, we knew we had done well. He was the toughest person I ever worked for, and the absolute best.

We finished up rehearsals and packed our things and caravanned to Missouri. The contract was for nine months. The theater was brand new and they still had quite a bit of work to do on it. It was beautiful, and the stage was huge. We started staging the show there, and it was almost like re-learning things. We had gotten so used to the studio, now we had the sets. I loved the production part of all of it. It was amazing to see how things came together, but it presented challenges at every turn. Even the lighting of the numbers was a big production. It would take Michael all night to light one number. We literally slept on the stage in our spots. The theater was pitch black. We couldn't even see him. We heard his voice in the microphone, and we made out the light from the tip of his cigarette as he inhaled.

"Please wake up and move to your next cue."

Sure enough, despite the challenges, when it came together, the show—a variety show with magic, dancing, singing, and even animal acts (much to the chagrin of PETA)—was beautiful. The choreography, costumes, props, sets, and lighting were unbelievable. How this could come from the mind of one man was just incredible. I will never forget the first time we were able to watch it (so he could help us point out our mistakes). We were blown away.

I loved the show, but the hour and a half drive to and from Branson every day to our lodgings in Springfield got old real quick. There was a show at 2 p.m. and 8 p.m. with four hours in between. We would get so bored. We usually slept between shows. I did make the mistake of smoking pot between shows once, and that was a horrible experience. How I made it through without falling off the stage I will never know. The show ended at 10 p.m., and by the time we returned to Springfield it would be last call at the bars so we didn't have much of a night life either. The cast was great, and we had fun together during rehearsals. We got really used to all hanging around each other. But once the show began, we had just one day off a week. The dance captains would swing other dancer's parts so the whole cast was never off on the same days. I was off with two people who were dating, so I spent a lot of time on my own. That got old really quick as well. You can only go to so many movies by yourself. Mind you, at my age now (and a mother of four), I would give anything for those moments of silence, but at this time there wasn't too much contemplation of the meaning of life going on for me. I was young and wanted to live it up.

About five months into the contract, a feud began between the stars of the show. First mistake: there cannot be *two* stars. This became quite apparent. Soon, both their dressing rooms were double bolted to keep the other one from entering. Because of the magic aspect of the show, there was a fear of sabotage. Seriously. The two of them were escorted to their dressing rooms and could never be in the hallway at the same time. I would compare it to a divorce, and the cast members were the children stuck in the middle. We had to choose between the two. We thought it was quite funny actually, watching these huge egos doing battle. The only problem was that we didn't want *either* of them. We thought they were utterly ridiculous. Their squabble got so bad that the show ended up closing at the seven month mark. The dancers were actually very happy with this decision. Seven months was enough.

Back to Vegas we went...but only for a minute.

A good friend of mine told me about auditions for a show called *Spellbound* that was playing at Harrah's in Vegas. I remember seeing pictures and was totally enamored by it. That show became my next goal and sure enough, when they had auditions to hire dancers for a world tour of the show, I went and booked it!

The contract was for one year. It would kick off in Seoul, Korea then would travel through twenty-seven cities in Germany and Switzerland. We would spend a few months in Lake Tahoe and

Atlantic City and finish in the Philippines. I was about to get paid to dance and travel the world.

How did I get from "Chickery Chick" to here? It was everything I had ever dreamed of and more. I was living out my fantasy.

Unfortunately, it wasn't enough.

I said it before, and I will say it again. If we don't get to the root of the problem, feel the pain it causes, accept whatever it is, and let it go...we will never be free. All the outside happiness does not take away the inside troubles. I was still in a battle with my own demons and insecurities. The voices never left, and when things spun out of control, I went back to the sure thing that I thought gave me the control.

And darkness followed...

CHAPTER 18
A DEAL WITH
THE DEVIL

There is a moment that I can remember, being on the beach in Raiatea, an island in French Polynesia, and looking out at the most beautiful water I had ever seen. I was on a break for the show after a couple weeks in Korea before heading out to Germany to start the tour. It was just me and another dancer, a close friend of mine. Everything about this short little excursion had been absolutely

magical. As I sat there looking out over the water, embracing the thrill of what my life had become, I was filled with this incredible sense of peace. It was wonderful.

I remember this moment because it was also one of the last times I would feel this way in a very long time.

Seoul itself had been surreal. Our group of twenty-five dancers had all become very close during rehearsals so at least we got to experience the stress and weirdness together as we spent our Christmas and New Year's there. I just remember it being so cold that we rarely went outside. When our host did take us out one evening, it was such an eerie feeling because no one was on the streets. They took us to this building that looked like...nothing. It was just a plain, nondescript building. We literally climbed through a huge open crack in a wall to go in, just enough to fit through. It turned out to be some underground club. The moment we walked in, all eyes were on us. We were there for fifteen minutes. I do not speak Korean, nor did any of the other dancers, but we could tell we were not welcome, and we were quickly escorted out. I didn't mind leaving Korea.

We had a quick break back in Vegas (and Polynesia for a couple of us!), then Munich, Germany for a month before kicking off a twenty-seven city tour. As thrilled as I was with the process and the show, I did once again deal with the pressure of feeling I had to look a certain way. And that's how some of the old insecurities came creeping back, and with them some very dangerous experiences, ones that could have changed my life, ones that still linger even today, and ones that sometimes, at my weaker moments, bring a sense of terror for my future.

We know that as dancers we have to keep a certain weight. What you are hired at, you stay at. That's it. Now you are always welcome to lose weight, but obviously not the other way around. During rehearsals they paired us up with someone who would be our opposite, kind of like a book end. So stage right and stage left would look even. My opposite was taller than me, and her body frame was more petite than mine. I was twelve pounds heavier. This was who I was compared to, which was not good for me.

What had started in middle school with controlling my weight and appearance had ever since been a part of my life. It fluctuated depending upon my moods, where I was in my life, and what I was doing, but it was always there. Over my dancing years I became more and more consumed with how my body looked. It came from the same place; controlling something when things in my life were spinning out of control.

My weight began to fluctuate, and the more energy I put into obsessing about it, the more of an issue it became. We had weekly weigh-ins. We would be called into the bathroom like cattle being herded. One by one, we hopped up on the scale. I was always let down. To make matters worse, during the tour we all had to share a hotel room. This made my "controlling habit" difficult to pull off. The less I could control this aspect of my life, the more obsessed I became about it.

I was always comparing, wanting, wishing to be a certain body type that I was not. It was always about the hip bones. Those damn skinny, protruding hip bones. In my mind, being that skinny would give me not just the control, but the self-worth I desired. Being skinny somehow made me a better person. Even writing this now, it doesn't feel or sound right. It's hard to put this mindset or obsession into words. I wish I could explain this in a way that made sense. I am so tempted to call it an addiction. I am sure some would agree and some would argue this statement. My defense would be that though it wasn't a substance I was addicted to, it was a habit, and it had a strong hold over me. I used to watch other people as they ate. I wondered what it would be like to just take a bite of something and not feel guilty. I honestly could not remember a time that I didn't feel shitty every time I ate something, and I mean *every* time. Basically if I was awake, I was consumed by it, and I craved any kind of way to stop obsessing.

That's where the trouble came from.

While traveling around to all the different cities, our only commitment was to show up for the shows and possibly a rehearsal now and then. Other than that, we were free to roam. That meant there were many nights out on the town. At one particular party, I kept noticing something going on in the corner of the room. People kept walking over and looking closely at something (or so I thought). Then they walked away with big smiles on their faces. I finally asked what they were doing. I was told they were snorting cocaine.

I had tried it in high school, but only a couple times. I felt totally uncomfortable even being around it.

But I didn't leave.

They explained that it wasn't that big of a deal. It just made you feel happy. They were pushing me to try a little. I was still hesitant when I remembered hearing something about how cocaine makes your appetite go away and how people who used it lost weight. It was like a light bulb turned on. If that were true, I could get out of my never-ending nightmare. It was at least worth a try.

That was at 10 p.m. At 7 a.m., I was still wide awake and feeling really good. I had so much energy and a feeling of euphoria. I'd also had nothing to eat. I did get a bloody nose, and I thought it was a little strange, but it was totally worth it because I wasn't hungry at all. Four weeks later, I was about twenty pounds lighter and experiencing pure happiness as I found myself in the throes of a serious cocaine addiction.

I had left the nightmare, but had made a deal with the devil.

Eating essentially stopped altogether. I was *really* skinny, and everyone noticed. But in the world of dance, that was the goal. The producer was complimenting me on how good I looked. He had even pointed me out in front of the other dancers, who I'm pretty sure all had a good idea what was going on.

Cocaine became my new obsession. All I could think about was how I could possibly keep this up. Believe me when I say, this was not just a "weekend" habit. My diet consisted of cocaine. Period. From the moment I woke up--if I had even gone to bed--I would start snorting and keep going throughout the day and into the night. All day, every day.

I loved the way I felt and looked. I had endless energy. It was amazing! And I could see no reason for it to end. I loved it; the producers loved it; I knew where to get it; and I had money. What could go wrong?

That was how I spent the next few months in Germany. As long as I had cocaine, life was good. As we neared the end of our time there, the plan was to head back to Vegas for a short break then off to Atlantic City for the summer. While I was packing my things to go back home, I realized I still had a lot of cocaine left. How could I waste this? There had to be a way to sneak it through customs. My bright idea was to seal it really well and put different packets in different hotel shampoo/conditioner bottles. I then put all the bottles in a plastic bag. That should be good through security X-ray machines. We arrived early at the airport and had a long wait before going through customs. There was a lot of back and forth going on in my mind. Of course, I had kept a little on me for the road so I was hitting the bathroom every twenty minutes or so. I mean, God forbid I start coming down before I get on the plane! As the line moved closer, I don't know how or why, but something struck me. I realized how incredibly dangerous this was. I took the baggie out of my luggage and, crossing my inner demons, I threw it out.

Once I got back home to Vegas, the challenge was finding more. Luckily in Vegas I did not have to look far. I bought $500 worth. I thought that would buy me a little time until I could find a hook up in Atlantic City...which I quickly did in some friends who were performing at a hotel downtown.

In Atlantic City, we were put up in some amazing condos on Brigantine Island, right on the beach. We were performing at Harrah's right over the bridge, which meant we had to rent cars and drive back and forth. One night, as I went to go see my friends perform and get my hookup, I got lost on the way home. There were areas in Atlantic City that were pretty dodgy, especially for a young girl driving around lost...with a tail light out. I drove down a one-way street. It was dark, and these men began to walk toward the car. I quickly threw it in reverse and was able to get back out on the main road just in time to notice a cop car behind me with the lights flashing. I pulled over.

Oh shit!

Two male police officers walked on each side of the car. I had the cocaine hidden in my underwear. I thought there was no way they weren't going to search me. I was done. But I stayed calm. Luckily I had not had any alcohol or used anything (yet) that night. The officers first asked me if I knew my taillight was out. Then they were questioning why I was in this particular area. I told them I had gotten lost. They continued with a few more questions, then gave me directions and recommended that I go straight home. All the while, I could feel the package of cocaine pressed against my body.

Unfortunately I did not learn from this. It was only one of many bad choices and close calls. At this point it was more than just about staying thin...I needed it.

And that's what has come with age, wisdom, reflection and... well, a lot of therapy. The eating disorder and the drug abuse were not the problem. They were what *stemmed* from the problem. Imagine the seed that gets planted in the ground. It sits for a long time. It begins to get nourished, and the more it's nourished the more it grows. Before you know it, a stem starts to make its way to the surface and out of the ground it grows. Buds begin to develop off of the stem. With all the different buds that develop, we tend to think those are the things we need to cut in order to keep from overgrowth. This is how we live our life.

It took years for me to realize what the original seed was made from.

Since my parents got divorced, that seed has grown. Who did I belong to? Who loved me? Who had my back?

Who was I?

The eating disorder was my own punishment for not being in

control. It was my punishment for not standing up for myself. It was my punishment for not being worthy.

The drugs were my escape. I was at a very low point personally, despite the façade the high gave me. Unfortunately, I still had a long way to go before hitting my rock bottom.

In general, Atlantic City for the summer was awesome...for a cocaine addict. I had plenty on hand. I had fallen hard, and my life totally revolved around my habit. My days and nights had now merged together. My roommates would have to wake me up around 5 p.m. to go to the show. That was the start of my day.

Then we were on to Lake Tahoe and that was a problem. I did not have any connections. Luckily, I was able to find someone in Vegas who could send it to me. It's amazing how clever people can be in coming up with creative ways to send drugs through the mail. I remember one time getting a magazine in the mail. Upon opening it, there was a perfectly clean rectangle cut into the pages. There it was fastened neatly inside. Despite this new hook-up, the cocaine never seemed to last.

Our contracts were set to expire soon. It had been a whole year, one long, drug-induced trip that melded together in a haze. The last leg of the tour would be in the Philippines. Since our contracts were up before the last leg, we could choose to finish and end our contracts in Tahoe or take the last trip. Sadly, I decided to end it. Why? I didn't know where I was going to get more cocaine over there. Although I spent a whole year with these people who had become my new family, unfortunately my bond with my addiction won out. Back to Vegas I went.

It was on this flight back I did one of the dumber things I've ever done and somehow (thank God) didn't get caught. Afraid of being without cocaine when I got back, I cut a little hole in my scrunchie and tucked a couple grams of cocaine in the fabric. Then I twisted my hair in it on top of my head. Looking back, I am still in awe at the power a drug addiction can wield.

Once I got back home, I realized how much being away from

the cast and crew affected me. I fell into a deep depression. I was so used to being with these people. I rarely felt alone while on tour. If I did, the solution was easy...walk out of my hotel room and knock on any other door on the floor. There was bound to be someone to hang out with. Now that was gone.

Luckily, soon after I returned, I was asked if I wanted a permanent spot in *Spellbound* on the Vegas Strip. Taking this show meant I could stay put for a while. It was not the ideal situation because half of the Las Vegas cast was fired and replaced by half of the cast that was on tour. So this was not the best transition into a show, and there was definitely no welcoming crew.

My partying continued, but that the euphoria feeling was harder to grasp. I needed more to get that feeling. The worst part of all was coming down. I still cringe thinking about this. I would fall into the deepest lows when the drug started to wear off, and it was happening quicker and quicker as my body actually built up an immunity to the drug. The sadness hit me like a truck. I felt it coming on and would panic, trying anything to avoid it. I would cry for hours and hours, unable to stop.

That was only the beginning.

The only solution appeared to be to take more, and that's when things got out of hand. Eventually it began to affect my responsibilities in the show. I was now forgetting choreography. I missed cues on stage, which then affected others, and they had to scramble and pick up the slack. I panicked before going on stage. My mind was completely blank, like I had never learned the dance before. I had to ask someone to show me the choreography right before going on. I was forgetting and losing everything, including leaving my credit card in the bathroom stall with a straw right next to it.

I also became a paranoid wreck.

It was nothing like it used to be. What once was so wonderful had now quickly and literally turned on me. The lows continued to get so bad that it almost got to a point of not being worth it for me. Almost. I wanted it too badly. I thought I could recapture that feeling. I kept needing more and more, but it wasn't working. I tried to stay away, but I was not strong enough to not do it. I would be up all night, staring at my image in the mirror, into my own eyes while snorting cocaine, but I saw nothing. I was completely taken over, yet I refused to believe that this person looking back was me. I lay alone in bed, staring at the ceiling, eyes as wide as saucers, begging to be able to fall asleep, promising myself that this would be the last time. My poor heart...it was nourished solely by this drug, constantly working overtime. I felt it pounding out of my chest. I was slowly killing myself.

How had this happened to me?

That's the key question and one every addict needs to ask before they can even think of getting better. Some of them never get the chance before tragedy hits. I consider myself one of the lucky few.

But am I?

CHAPTER 19
IF ONLY IT WERE THAT EASY

My revelation came late one night in Vegas, as I sat in complete darkness.

For the first time in months, if not ever, I got a moment of clarity about how difficult all of this was--the scoring, the hiding, the toll on the body, the need, the want, the crave, the pain, the coming down, the emotional hurt, the obsession, the utter destruction of a once innocent little girl with big dreams and lots of love to give.

I couldn't do it anymore.

Depressed, lonely, and scared, I called my friend Amy. We had been through so much together during middle school and high school. She was always my rock. I felt safe with her. Years had passed, but I knew we could take right back up where we left off. I told her everything. That was the only way. I had to be truthful. If not, there was no point and I wouldn't get the help I needed.

I think she was in shock, and very disappointed as well. Mainly, though, she was scared for me. She cried, and I remember being so taken aback by this. She begged me to get help, and threatened to call my mother if I didn't. I promised her I would.

If only it were that easy.

I am only speaking from my experience, but I think that this is where a person teetering on the edge decides to take the fall. I do not know what it was, but something kept me from this fall. I think. Maybe lying there in my bed, listening to my heart race and staring off into the void *was* taking that fall. Trust me when I say I teetered on the brink of what could have been the next step, at least what I think the real fall would be, only to pull myself back.

While I have been focusing on cocaine, I need to come completely clean and mention the others. Acid, ecstasy, crystal meth, crack...I tried them all. I had already proven to have an addictive personality and craved both the euphoria and the numbing of my life so I very easily could have gotten hooked on any one of them as well. Somehow I didn't go down that path. Cocaine was my favorite because it allowed me to, for the most part at least, keep dancing. Despite where my drug-addled brain was at the time, dancing was still important to me.

So I was lucky to never fall into that pit. Still, the cocaine addiction was enough. Quitting was no overnight job. Although strength and determination were one hundred percent necessary, without will, I would have been hopeless.

The first thing I had to do was break the ties. This was very difficult as my friends were my world. We supported each other's journey. During the all-nighters, we kept each other company. During the lows, we had the misconception that we were helping each other. Still, they were reflective of this life, this addiction. They were part of it and for it to go, they had to go. Since we were not at the same place, I had to be strong and simply not hang around them. This caused major turmoil between all of us. Things even got a little evil. It was scary because we saw a different side of each other. And of course the moment I decide to be done with it, it was constantly being offered to me. I could not get away from it. It followed me everywhere. Like a shadow, always behind me, tapping on my shoulder.

This meant a lot of starting and stopping. I would be good, avoid it, and then, inevitably I would fall. I would swear that it was the last time. I would be good and then I would fall again. This happened for a year. Luckily between each fall, the time I spent clean increased.

After that year, I left *Spellbound*. I thought maybe a fresh start with new surroundings would help. I auditioned and took a job in Tokyo, Japan. We would be there for three months. But after just one month, I fell back in. It somehow always found me, or rather I found it.

I knew I was going nowhere but down. I felt horrible. Here I was, now in a country where I couldn't even come close to speaking the language, constantly facing the fear of being caught and locked up abroad. I found myself at huge rave parties in the middle of nowhere, in these huge abandoned buildings, with people I had just met, high out of my mind. How I survived is beyond me. I don't believe it was luck, I just think...I don't know what I think. I just know that something worse happening to me wasn't in the cards. Still, I was caught in the downward spiral. I had to get out of Japan. I was under the influence of cocaine the rest of the contract, up to the moment I got on the plane to return to the US.

I was heading back home, but I was still lost. The difference, though it didn't do anything to stop me at the time, was that now I *knew* I was lost.

To make things even more interesting, when I came back to Vegas, I met up with an old friend who popped up to make my life just a bit more complicated, even if just for an evening.

Yep. Cal.

Somehow, Cal and I had kept in touch. Cal and I never discussed anything right after the suicide attempt. We were friendly with each other. Honestly, at this point, I just wanted to be friends with him. In a way, I wanted to be sweet as pie and keep his friendship so I could prove to him he hadn't broken me. I always had an underlying desire to rub my success in his face, that I could leave home, become a dancer. Yet I still wanted his acceptance.

Obsession is an interesting creature.

Then Cal complicated things by moving to California about a year after me. I have stories of us meeting up over the years, but it never ended well. Then we wouldn't talk for a long time, then somehow we would meet up again. There was a significant meeting when I was dancing in the *Spellbound* world tour, in that short break before I went to Germany. Right before I went on the trip to Polynesia with my friend, I met up with Cal in L.A. The day was weird. I'm not sure if he was into drugs yet but he was hanging around some strange people, and he took me with them wandering around to different places in L.A. I remember feeling very uncomfortable around these people. We ended up going to dinner and back to his house in Malibu and ended up having horrible sex. It was just like old times, me caving in to satisfy him and him only. Then I felt bad, and it snowballed when we experienced an earthquake. We were lying there, the bed shaking, and all I could think of was sliding down the cliff where Cal's house was perched. I started getting nervous and angry. At some point I listened to a message that had been left on my phone, and it was my mom telling me my great grandmother had passed. I was freaking out because I couldn't tell my mom where I was as I didn't want her to know I was with Cal. I was upset about my great grandmother, and he couldn't console me in any way. Instead, he went into the bathroom and locked the door. I began pounding on the door telling him to come out, but he wouldn't. I went and found the fuse box and shut the power off. He came out. I was yelling at him. I told him I was going to leave. Unfortunately he didn't try to stop me, not even for a second. I was hoping he would because I didn't know anyone, it was late at night, and I had nowhere to go. But no, so I left.

That was a rather average Cal and Kori interaction.

I met up with him again from time to time in Vegas. I don't know why.

When I returned from Japan, I was hired to do a show called *Viva Las Vegas* which was a day show. At the same time I was hired to do a show called *Gone Country* which had two evening shows. This was perfect, as I was so busy. I never had a day off, just a day that I would be doing two shows instead of four. My weight was slowly creeping back to "normal" standards because I was actually eating. I was feeling very self-conscious, but it was good. I had no time to mess around anymore. Nor did I want any part of it. The goal was just to stay far away from anyone and anywhere I could get into trouble.

It was during this time I got set up on a blind date with a guy named Sam. He was fifteen years older, which didn't bother me. We went out and had a nice time and pretty soon after, we started dating. I really wanted no part of a relationship, and I had so many other issues I was trying to tackle, but something pushed me into it.

Even after all this time, I still craved love and stability.

Something was always a little off in my gut, but nonetheless I liked him. It somehow felt comfortable, almost like I knew him. Although at the time I was not aware, I realized later that the comfort was more of a feeling of...*home*. And that's because Sam reminded me of my father. In fact, he practically *was* my father.

We dated for about a year, and it was a rocky relationship. There were trust issues. I never quite knew how honest he was being with me. I never could have imagined being with him long term; the red flags were everywhere. He even told me a story about him cheating on his ex-wife and actually said these words to me.

"My wife could walk in a room and catch me cheating on her and I could still lie my way out of it."

The straw that broke the camel's back hit way too close to home. One evening the plan was for him to pick me up after work outside the backstage door. I waited and waited. For two hours to be exact. I was calling him, and he never picked up his phone. I was stranded because I didn't have a car and all the dancers had left. Even after all the disappointments and the lack of follow-through with my father, I still always gave him the benefit of the doubt. The same went for Sam; I just knew something must have happened to him. There was no way he would just leave me there. Well, something did happen...he was having drinks with his ex-fiancé and he forgot about me. That was that.

But while I was with Sam, Cal came to visit and saw me in *Viva Las Vegas*. It was crazy having Cal in the audience actually. Later on, we all went to dinner together. I'm not sure how it started, but Sam was messing with Cal, just teasing, and he got pissed. I was in the women's restroom, and Cal came barreling in, screaming about anything and everything before storming out. That began yet another period of silence with Cal.

During the Sam experiment, I was actually starting to clean up my act when it came to the drug use. By this time I had bought a little house, and I really enjoyed being home. Don't get me wrong, traveling was awesome, but I needed stability in my life, or I tended to get myself in trouble.

After my *Gone Country* contract expired, I took a role in the long-running *Jubilee*, which was an incredible and mesmerizing production. Each act told a different story. One was about Samson and Delilah, another one was about the sinking of the Titanic. The closing act was so elegant. Imagine Fred Astaire and Ginger Rogers in black tie and gown. For those moments on stage, I felt like a movie star back in the early 1900s. Let's not forget

to mention the finale number with the most amazing costumes. You have never seen so much sparkle on one stage. Just like a snowflake, no two costumes were the same.

Remember when I was living with Momoo and Dadoo and I had my closet and my secret hidden box with the imaginary jewels? Well, when I was hired, I was not one of the girls who wore one of the extravagant finale costumes. Not everybody did. I was a little bummed, but no big deal. When I was six months in though, they had a spot open, and I was chosen to fill it. I didn't know which costume I would get. But there were three different groups of costume colors. Yep, ruby, emerald, and sapphire...just like my jewels! The dresser walked me back to the room where they housed all of them. To this day I can remember him opening the door to the room. There, right in front of me, was my costume. This time it was not in my imagina-

tion. I would be drenched in the most beautiful emerald stones I had ever seen. The headdress alone weighed around thirty pounds. It wrapped down and around and connected at my waist. It was almost like I stepped inside the jewel. Like an ornament. It was magical. Not strange, not bizarre, not weird. Magical!

I was very honored to be a part of the cast and this production.

One other major plus... there were no weigh-ins! The producer loved women to look like women as opposed to stick figures. So hips and boobs were a good thing. I had just a little less pressure, which was exactly what I needed.

Things were good. I was able to keep my head on straight and stay away from the big C. That being said, I had to be careful because the feeling was never too far away. I had once read about the effects of alcohol on a recovered alcoholic. Even after being sober for years, if he or she falls off, they will pick up right where they left off. Like no time had passed. I didn't understand this. During my process of becoming clean, I wouldn't touch cocaine for months. I was under the impression I could handle it because it had been so long. I thought the effects would go back to the euphoria feeling. I could not have been more wrong. It never came back.

I had to avoid anything having to do with it. If ever I was in the same room with this drug, I had to leave; the room was not big enough for the both of us. I believe after twenty years, if I would partake, I would be right back where I was at the height of my drug use. What was even crazier was how much my sleep was affected even years after not touching this drug. This was my first lesson on the power of the mind.

I literally would have to be in bed by 10 p.m. If it got much past this time, I would begin to feel the effects of cocaine. I would start to panic, and I would lie awake in bed for hours. Again, this affected me for years.

Dealing with the drug addiction and the eating disorder was not easy. I had to realize that they don't go away; you just choose not to interact with them. They will always be a part of my life, danger-ously so. I have learned how to live cohesively with them. They are like roommates. I have to get along with them and have an adult relationship with them, or I suffer the consequences. As humans, we need to get to the source of the problem. No more excuses. We can't change things unless we find our truth and confront it. If we believe we are not worthy of someone or something good, then we will never be worthy of someone or something good. Our past events may shape us. But they are not who we are. It is all a facade. Until we realize this, we will always return to the surface.

When I think back on my life, what is interesting to me was that I refused to believe I ever fell victim to these things. I never believed I was raped. I never believed I had an eating disorder. I never believed I was addicted. To me, I was not worthy of these so called titles. I still refuse to believe. I am not any of these things; they do not make me who I am. These things do not make me anything other than stronger for not being taken down by them. I did fight for a long time, but in the end I won! Or at least, I'm winning.

Part of the reason why is because of the man I was about to meet.

CHAPTER 20
CLINT

I could write an entire book about that man, and in many ways, that's exactly what I'm doing as there is no single person who has impacted my life more. He is the reason for this tale, for my opening up to the world and myself. In fact, as I said earlier, he's the one who actually *is* writing this book. I feel him guiding me now as he has since we first fell in love with each other and while I continue to miss him each and every day, I always feel him here with me. Without Clint, I don't know where my story would have taken me.

But I do know I would have never been brave enough to share it.

This point in my story marks the beginning of the happiest time in my life leading up to the worst time in my life. My never-ending quest to not only pick myself up and stay on the true path ahead of me, but to thrive in the journey and be my best self. The strength comes from the memory and the powerful, loving presence of my one and only soul mate.

I'm getting ahead of myself. I haven't even really introduced him yet. So let's go back to Vegas as I remember how it started with a smile on my face and warmth in my heart.

I was then twenty-seven years old. I had a mortgage payment and a dog, and I was doing what I loved to do. My life was pretty much on track or at least getting better. Just one thing seemed to be missing: a relationship. But after my last escapade, I was actually fine with that. I was comfortable being single, focusing on myself, and not worrying about finding love and stability in the arms of a man.

That is usually when it happens, isn't it?

Meeting Clint was pretty unlikely and even a little ironic in more ways than one. First, I was out with the same friend who set me up on the blind date with Sam, so I didn't exactly associate her with good luck when it came to men, at least not for me. We were going to Spago, which was located in the Caesar's Palace Forum Shops. When we arrived, they were packed and there was an hour wait so we decided to leave...

...and go to the Cheesecake Factory.

Ugh.

There was no wait, and they brought us to our table right away. On the way, we walked by a table where two guys were seated. I was immediately drawn to one of them, and we caught eyes for a moment. I kept walking and noticed I didn't feel the presence of my friend behind me any longer. I stopped and looked back and as it turned out, she had stopped to talk to them. She knew them. I went back to their table, and she introduced us. We chatted for a couple minutes and then we went and sat at our table.

I had a hard time not looking at the one I was drawn to...Clint. It wasn't just that he was handsome (he was!), it was that he had this energy about him, something exuded from him that I found so attractive. I could tell right away that he was funny and charming. Even though he was a bigger guy, I could also tell he was sweet and had a sensitive side. I felt connected to him, and I don't mean that to sound creepy as I know I didn't know him. There was just something happening right away, and he would later tell me he felt it too. It's always hard to put that level of attraction, that feeling, that sense of something bigger happening into words, but it moved me. Although I did not mention this to my friend, the whole time I couldn't stop thinking about him. Much to my delighted surprise, they finished eating and joined us. Along with Clint was his friend Bryan, who would become a good friend of mine eventually. In fact, Bryan would be the one to say a few words about Clint at the paddle out that got everyone splashing the water in that magical moment. They stayed the entire time, and we walked out together.

That's when it happened, the moment I will never, ever forget. It would be the first of many moments that would come to define our relationship and truly, the moment I think I fell in love with Clint. We had been flirting, and so we exchanged numbers. As we said goodbye to each other, he gave me the most amazing hug I had ever received. I know some would say it's just a hug, but again, it's tough to describe the power. In writing this book, I think of all the love, stability, comfort I had been seeking in all the wrong places over the course of my young life.

I found all of it in that hug.

He was the warmest comforter on the coldest day and that hug was all it took. The spark was lit, and it soon became a tiny flame and then a roaring fire.

When we come across a good one, some people tend to take more time to strategize. They need to have a good action plan to make sure nothing gets messed up. Well, I've never really been one to follow the plan. We all are aware of the three-day rule. God forbid we look needy or show excitement too soon. Clint was on the three-day rule plan, but I wasn't. I did ponder the idea of waiting, but it just wasn't going to happen. It was the next morning, while I was heating my coffee in the microwave. It beeped, and I thought screw it, I'm calling.

Or should I? Why not? Is that too soon? Why wait? I can be the bigger person! But should you be or should you leave it to him? What do I have to lose? What if it scares him off?

If calling two days early is going to break the relationship then I guess it is not meant to be.

Yep, so I picked up the phone and called him. He answered. No weirdness. We planned a date!

Thursday, October 9, 1997. That was our first date. We didn't do anything mind-blowing. Of course I don't think he would appreciate that comment. I had just one show that evening, and I went to his house afterwards. He met me at the front door. His house was so clean and organized, which for me left a great second impression. We simply sat and talked most of the night.

The love drug hit me and hit me hard. I was bursting with energy for what this was very quickly becoming. I was entranced by him. He was so funny, so full of happy, positive energy! The way he told stories could suck you in like a vacuum! He was so alive, so boisterous!

I'm sorry about all the exclamation marks, but truth be told, he deserves more. That's the kind of energy that Clint was made of and showed the world. That's the energy I fell in love with on our first date.

Of course, the old doubts came creeping back in right away. In fact, I had one thought eating away at me: Can I fool this guy?

I thought he was so out of my league, and I was determined to not let him find out who I really was; it wasn't safe. After all, I was not class president, I was not homecoming queen, I was not voted most popular. At Clint's Tucson high school,  he *was* student body president, homecoming king, and yes, captain of the football and basketball teams. In my mind, I was not worthy of someone of this stature. It hurts to realize there was a time I felt this way about myself, especially with a man who would come to love me unconditionally, but it was my truth at the time. And so I reverted back to my old mantra: Fake it 'til you make it.

The definition of that phrase reads, "By imitating confidence, competence, and an optimistic mindset, a person can manifest those qualities in their real life."

It is that simple...believe in yourself. I was struggling to do that right from the start, but I was going to push myself to do so and hope and pray the cards would turn in my favor.

Within the first week of our date, Clint came to see the show. He was supposed to go to the snack bar near the theater. That was where my favorite security guard and lifetime friend Officer Randy would meet all the guests who were friends of the cast members. He then would escort them up to the light booth. Before the show the dancers could make a quick stop to say hello. I remember being so excited that he was there to see the show. We had a mandatory warm-up onstage every night, and I could barely stand it. I put my makeup on and got my pre-sets ready as quickly as I could, so I would have time to go up and say hello.

As I climbed the stairs, the old fears crept in again. The thought did cross my mind that maybe he would not be there. I got a sinking feeling in my gut, and as I walked through the door, I prepared myself for the familiar disappointment. I steeled myself for it...but there he was. He walked toward me with the biggest grin on his face, all his big, tall beauty. And he was there to see *me!*

There had to be at least sixty to seventy dancers on stage at once during the different acts. I know he was pretty proud of himself because he said he was able to point me out every time...which of course, probably wasn't possible, but Clint would sometimes embellish his stories.

I did find out he was also not a fan of the "showgirl" make-up with the big lashes and the red lips. I had to explain I would look faceless from the audience without the exaggerated features. This actually led to a funny realization during a conversation one day. Not only was the first house Clint owned within a couple blocks of mine, he also managed a restaurant called Roxy's in the Stratosphere , when I was dancing in a show there. He recalled being in the cafeteria when the dancers would walk in with all our makeup on. We definitely were not discreet. "I wonder what jerks these girls date?" was what he thought at the time.

I told him that I guess he got his answer.

Soon after, I had the opportunity (with the help of my mother) to buy the house in which I had rented a room from Toni. She got engaged and was moving to California. Although we didn't know it then, this would be mine and Clint's first home together as a married couple. My mother had flown out to help me move, and this was the first time she would meet Clint.

I honestly don't think she knew what to expect after my previous relationship. Clint had her at hello! She never stopped laughing from his hilarious stories and I can honestly say she was mesmerized by him. There was never that uncomfortable awkwardness that sometimes can happen when you first meet someone. Then again, what was not to like?

Clint was everything I had sought after and dreamed about in a man. I was learning rather quickly that this man was full of incredible qualities. He was hilarious, consistently calm, and always prepared. It was near impossible to catch him off guard. He was charismatic and enigmatic. It wasn't just me who was drawn to him; it was *everybody.* He loved the spotlight and telling stories that would grow based on the size of his audience. He always smiled.

He was genuinely a happy person and I hadn't encountered too many of those in my young life.

I was finally in a position to look to the future with hope and a smile...something that hadn't happened in a long time. Best of all, he was in love with me. I started planning our future.

Now I just needed to make sure I didn't lose him!

CHAPTER 21
OPERATION
PROPOSAL

Within the first few months of our courtship, Clint started training for a triathlon. One night in conversation I asked him what he would do if I did the triathlon with him. Without hesitation he answered, "I would be so impressed I would propose to you at the finish line."

My reply, "Game on!"

Ok, as a mother, I know that when you make a promise to child, no matter the reason, if it's something they want, they'll hold you to it. That's why you have to be careful with what you say. Well, out came my inner child, and Clint could instantly tell that I was not only going to do this triathlon but hold him to his promise.

That was day one of Operation Proposal.

Now came the hard part: Training. Ironically enough, I got a jump on it a couple days later when I went to a health food store looking to buy some protein powder. I randomly befriended the man working behind the counter and ended up coming home with a ten-speed road bike from the 1970s. He just let me have it! I remember Clint's comment when he saw me getting the bike out of the car. "Only you Kori...you ask about protein powder and end up with a bike!"

Before I go any further, I should probably mention that although I had been on the swim team for years, I had not done much biking, and I was *not* a distance runner. This would be my first triathlon. I wasn't even sure how to begin training for something like this. There was definitely a lack of confidence when telling friends I was training for the "Escape from Alcatraz" triathlon in San Francisco. But I have never been one to turn down a challenge...especially with this kind of a deal at hand.

We trained together for a little over a month. I really wasn't concerned about the swimming part--I was more concerned about the temperature of the water. We needed wetsuits, so I purchased one and he borrowed one, and we kept up with the swimming training as well as the running. I also continued to train on the 1970s road bike. Besides it skipping gears every now and then when I needed to peddle hard up a hill, it seemed to work just fine. I was beginning to think I could do this!

It was a couple days before we were leaving for San Francisco, and I was coming down with something. I'm sure some of this was mental. Either way I didn't want to chance it so I called in sick to *Jubilee*. My roommate was coaxing me to go, but I just was not feeling it. It turns out the dancers had bought a huge cake and had previously gotten together to take some hilarious pictures

of themselves mocking Clint and I doing the triathlon. It was all laid out on a big poster board. It was so sweet of them, and I was kicking myself for not going in that night, but I had bigger things on my mind. I was going to race. I was going to finish. I was going to get engaged.

The next day we were on our way. After we checked into the hotel, we headed to the race meeting. They explained how the day would go and showed us the swim, bike, and run routes. That's when the nerves started kicking in. There would be seven hundred of us put on a barge to Alcatraz. We would jump off the barge to start because the area around the island was not conducive for that. The bike route didn't  seem so bad when we drove the route, but that's probably because we were *driving* it. And the run was only nine miles, so that wasn't so bad, right?

Back at the hotel, Clint pulled me aside and began to show me how to change a flat bike tire. I stared at him with big deer eyes, questioning why he waited until the night before the race to show me this. The thought of getting a flat tire never even crossed my  mind. After that lesson I pretty much told myself that if I got a flat, the race would be done for me. Part of me thought it was a ploy on his part...I think he was nervous that I may just beat him! Well, Clint got his though, when he realized he should have probably tried on the wetsuit he had borrowed. I am assuming it didn't dawn on him that whoever you borrow a wet suit from should have a body comparable to your own. Clint was six-foot-three and quite built. The wetsuit was clearly designed for someone five-foot. I am not sure how he even got it on. Thank god for vasoline.

At the crack of dawn the next morning, we all loaded onto the boat to take us to Alcatraz. There was not much talking going on. I may have had a couple of nervous tears get stuck in my goggles, but Clint wasn't aware. They prepared us on the way out. We were informed that as soon as they opened the back doors we had to jump in. They had to get all seven hundred of us off quickly. The way we were all stuffed in, I felt like we were cattle shuffling together, being herded to the edge. Some rules I am really good at following, so when I got to the edge, with no hesitation, I took one last glance at Clint and then...

I jumped in.

I instantly felt my body cringe as the coldness of the water entered my wetsuit. I took one look around, and Clint was nowhere to be found. I put my head down and began swimming. It didn't take long for the mass of people to spread out. The plan was to swim across the current as quick as possible to the other side and then swim with the current until we ended up at Krissy Park where we would transition to the bikes.

When I got to Krissy Park and tried walking out of the water, it became quite apparent how cold the water was. I couldn't move my fingers. I remember trying to say something, but I couldn't move my mouth. Our bikes were all set up in an area kind of far away, with the idea being to make people run a little to get the blood flowing properly again. This was actually very smart because even after the run I still had a hard time tying my shoe-laces as my fingers were still not moving very well.

I had not seen Clint since the boat, so I assumed he was long gone. I grabbed my 1970s road bike and took off for the hills. My bike didn't want to cooperate. Just as in training, I had to peddle exceptionally hard or stand up out of my seat when going uphill just to get it going, and often my gears would skip and the chain would jump. The problem was that I had nineteen miles of this. I hadn't thought this through properly. Oh well, suck it up, buttercup!

Or not.

Halfway up the first climb, the bike skipped about four gears and the chain just popped off. Now this wasn't good. I had only practiced fixing a flat tire, not putting a chain back on. This was all Clint's fault! I flipped the bike over, and to the best of my ability started trying to get the chain back on. As I was in my own frantic little world working profusely to get it back on, I heard a very recognizable voice coming from behind me.

"Hey baby, do you need help?" I immediately turned my head around, in what I'm sure looked like the pivotal scene out of *The Exorcist*. I cannot remember the words I said, but it was very clear that I wasn't going to take any of his help. It was also at that very moment that it dawned on me...

 I WAS AHEAD OF HIM!

Now I was pissed. That anger must have worked in my favor because I somehow got the chain popped back on and got back in the race!

The rest of the bike portion was pretty uneventful, and I actually found myself enjoying it. Now, onto the nine-mile run. This would have been fabulous had it not involved a quick jaunt down to the beach which led to a 250-foot sand stairwell. By the time I arrived, the stairs had disappeared and what I saw in front of me was a 250-foot sand wall. When I finally reached the top, with just few feet left, I literally had a hand on each thigh, physically lifting my legs one at a time because they felt like cement blocks.

But I could see the finish line.

Oh my god, I can totally see it! I cannot believe this. I really am going to finish this thing!

And who would you guess was standing, waiting for me at the finish line? Clint with his big, beautiful grin, beaming with pride. Our final scores were:

CLINT 3:12:19

KORI 3:28:05

Ok, so let's cut to the chase. Apparently, I really caught him off guard. I guess he wasn't prepared for me to finish. We were still new enough at dating so that he was unaware of my determination and once I have something on my mind...all bets are on. So no, he did *not* propose to me at the finish line. Even after all that! Was I disappointed? Actually, no I was not. I honestly didn't think he would that day. We hadn't been dating that long. I was also not concerned. I knew in my heart that he would one day and that it would be amazing. There was not a doubt in my mind.

The Alcatraz triathlon ended up being such an amazing experience for me. I loved every minute of it. Unfortunately, I loved it so much that I have never done another triathlon. I was afraid nothing would compare to it. Instead I ended my triathlete career on what I thought was a high note.

Clint and I returned to Vegas. He was managing Bertolini's restaurant in the Forum Shops at Caesars Palace, and my show *Jubilee* became home for me. I was so happy in my relationship with Clint. The thought of going back out on the road was not something that interested me anymore. And so we settled into our relationship.

There was a beautiful April day. In fact, it was April 15 to be exact. Clint and I were actually getting ready to head back to Ohio for my friend Heather's wedding. She had asked me to be a bridesmaid. Although I was looking forward to having Clint meet everyone, I was still at least a little irritated that I would be introducing him still as my "boyfriend."

As I walked in to the theater, my normal routine would be to stop at the corridor before entering and talk to Officer Randy. He listened patiently as I whined to him about my irritation. I guess I rambled on for quite some time because I didn't notice that the dancers were already on the stage for the mandatory warm up that takes place at the same time every night. Linda, our company manager, came up and reprimanded me for not being on stage. I didn't see what the big deal was, but I scurried over to join the cast with my tail between my legs.

It may have been five minutes before Linda came back out on stage to have us all huddle up for a company meeting. I remember hearing some deep breaths coming from the other dancers. I suddenly got nervous, trying to imagine what this could be about. We were always in fear of the show closing or losing our jobs.

As I was sitting there I couldn't help but notice out of the corner of my eye this beautiful man. He was dressed up so sharp in a suit and tie and he came walking across the stage. As he approached I couldn't believe my eyes!

Why was Clint here?

He introduced himself and without missing a beat he continued to rattle off the years, months, weeks, days, hours, even up to the very minute and back to the very moment we had met. He then said, and I quote, "All those moments bring me to this moment, where I will get down on this knee and ask that she share the rest of her moments with me."

I am pretty sure he didn't know what hit him after that! I practically knocked him over as I jumped on top of him and gave him the biggest kiss. I was beyond surprised, and couldn't believe he pulled this off! I did not have a clue! It was the most amazing proposal I could have imagined and again all that I had ever dreamed of, just like this man.

While we were reminiscing later, he actually told me how long he had been planning this. For months he had been hiding the ring in different spots around the house hoping I would never see it. He originally spoke with Linda about his grandiose idea to see if he could propose during the show. He asked if he could possibly be rigged up somehow and come flying in onto center stage from one of the high up rafters. Clint loved to capture an audience!

Well, he caught me. And this would now be the start of the most amazing time of my life. First comes love, then comes marriage, then comes...

CHAPTER 22
SO MANY
HAPPY TIMES

I realize now that I'm getting closer and closer to the pivotal moment in my life. I'm getting close to that loss, that love that was stripped away from me, that familiar slide into a darker place, and the mad scramble to hold on and push myself out of it. It's harder to think of now more than any other point in creating this book as I reflect on the joy, comfort, peace, happiness, and love, so

much love that I experi-enced in my brief but full time with Clint and the family we would create together. It's difficult for me to comprehend how the worst moment in my life could come during the best time in my life, but that's just how it works sometimes. All you can do is be grateful that you at least have those happy times and appreciate them for what they were.

And we had so many happy times.

After a year and a half of dating, we got engaged and then about another year and a half later, in 2000, we got married. I pulled it off; I had fooled him. Clint Clausen, the popular, athletic, outgoing, hilarious, charismatic man wanted to marry me. I just knew he would be an amazing husband and father and we would build a family and it would be the family life I had always dreamed about.

It was.

Of course, as in any relationship, it was like riding a roller coaster. We had our ups, and we had our downs. But most importantly we had each other and we wouldn't have had it any other way.

Clint had the ability to make me feel at ease no matter what the situation. I would go to him in a panic many times, and he could always put the fire out in one quick calm conversation. That's how he handled things, and I soon found that was something I needed more than anything else in my life. He didn't panic or stress or complain about things. He was so loving and didn't have a problem showing it. He would listen and somehow he could deal with my oddities, doing and saying just the right things to comfort me. If I was sad, all he had to do was take me in his arms and that feeling of security would soothe me. He was my protector of all things.

He was what my father never was. It wasn't until I met Clint that I realized that despite my own strength and determination, I also sometimes needed protection...even from myself.

Clint would also makes jokes about everything, and I mean *everything*! I think he thought of himself as a stand-up comic, but while he could always put on an act, his life was anything but. He was a generally happy man who just found himself able to laugh at the absurdity of life. I would get so annoyed and question how he could make a joke about such serious things. Upon hearing a comment he would make I would reply, "You can't say that!", he would reply back to me, with a big grin on his face, "I just did" then walk away laughing. I later came to the realization that whatever the circumstance, though we have to feel and experience the pain, hurt, sorrow, we then have to let it go or it will consume us. So if laughing at something can take away the *energy* that surrounds that feeling, then so be it. That's what Clint would do. I even think sometimes that somehow, in his own way, Clint would have found the circumstances of his own death something to laugh about. For some reason, that brings me peace.

He also had a tremendous work ethic. A few months before we were married, we moved to Chicago. At the time I was in *Jubilee* and was a massage therapist at the Mirage for a bit. A friend of the family lived there and was starting up a mortgage company, and he asked Clint if he wanted to learn the business and help out. I had been in the show for two years, and I didn't enjoy massaging at the spa. So when the idea was proposed, I was totally on board. At this point, as I approached our wedding date, I was starting to think more about starting a family than I was about dancing. I really felt that I had accomplished what I set out to do with my dancing career and I felt fulfilled with that. I was not concerned about the move because I was with him. We moved to Chicago, and he worked his butt off on learning a whole new business... never *once* complaining. He just did what he needed to do.

We were there for fourteen months. The gray and the cold were wearing on me, and I had a nanny job that I loved, but I wanted more. Honestly, I wanted a family of my own. I wanted to go back to Vegas so badly but I knew how hard he had worked and the business was just starting to take off. We had a discussion. I said I needed to know if we were staying for good because I had to change my outlook and learn how to cope. He said we were going to stay. I cried for a while and then said ok. It obviously had an effect on him because the next day he told me to start packing. We were a team, and he wanted me happy. I was his first priority, and I always remembered and cherished that about him.

We got back to Vegas and moved back into our house. I was going to be hired back into *Jubilee*. When I went backstage one day for a costume fitting, I remember not feeling comfortable. I assumed it was that old familiar feeling of seeing myself in that costume and not being happy with what I saw. I felt really bloated and a little nervous.

It turns out I was pregnant.

In the beginning of our relationship, the topic of kids and how long I would want to wait to have them once I was married came up. I discussed with him the five-year plan. I knew very well that there was no way in hell I was going to adhere to this. But for the sake of not wanting him to feel any pressure or to scare him off, this was what I told him. After a year and a half of dating, which ultimately led to a proposal, I thought, *Well, he is halfway in, maybe negotiations would be open for a three-year plan.* Then, as we approached our wedding date, I wondered if he even remembered the five-year plan or if it was possible to shorten it. I planned a strategy for how to break this to him and more importantly, get him on board. So this brings us to our wedding night. By this point there was no turning back, and as we were lying there talking about how great the evening had been, I gave him a long stare. Without any hesitation, I blurted out, "Well, about that five-year plan. Wouldn't you agree there is no better time than the present?"

He agreed!

It is interesting because I always loved the thought of babies and always dreamed of being pregnant and having my own, but I was so afraid because of all the dysfunction and craziness that went on in my family. That really turned me off to the idea of a large family until I met Clint and literally observed the interactions with his brother and sisters. They honored each other and loved hanging out together, and suddenly I realized that a family would be whatever we made it.

I thought about what a great father he would be. I literally thought more about having a baby after he proposed than I did about the wedding. I was ready to begin trying on our honeymoon. Just like with most things, when I get it in my head, there is a serious determination that kicks in. I was on a mission! In fact, one time I made him pull the car over because I was ovulating and we had a four-hour drive to wherever we were going. We had to do it right then!

It took a long, slow, impatient year...but it happened.

I was ecstatic! I absolutely loved being pregnant. It was actually the only time in my life I felt *good* about having a belly!

And because I like a challenge, and I need to prove I can do what I set out to do, I decided I wanted to have our first one at home. Now there are a couple reasons for this. One, I thought my doctor was a little too eager to call for a c-section; she seemed to have many patients who had them and it was much easier to set a date for that then to wait for the unpredictability of going into labor. Two, I had felt this hard bump under my rib cage for quite a few months, and I kept telling my doctor I thought it was the head, that I possibly had a "breach baby." She never agreed with me...until the last month when she looked at me and said, "Your baby is breach, we will probably have to schedule a c-section."

You don't say.

Obviously, I wasn't happy so she said she could try to turn her. We would have to go to the hospital, they would give me something to relax my muscles, and she could maneuver the baby by pressing and pushing on my stomach until the head was down. I told Clint the day we went in for this, "If this works, we are having her at home." Now, nine times out of ten it doesn't work... but guess what!

I was already seeing a midwife anyway. I wanted a natural birth without epidural because I had read if they give it wrong they could hit a nerve which could cause migraines that could last for months! That scared the crap out of me, so no epidural. I did actually have her at home, which was by far the most difficult and painful thing I have ever done. But that is why they call it labor. It was the longest night of my life, and after that I told Clint he was never allowed to call me a wimp again. Although no epidural became my goal, my next three births were in a hospital.

Clint had always wanted five kids, just like his family. I didn't have a number, but I knew after the first pregnancy, I wanted more and I wanted them rather close together. We gave birth to our first child in 2002 and by 2008 we had four.

Four daughters.

I found this hysterical. I would tease him by saying, "I don't know what you did in college, but payback's a..." and I would walk away laughing.

I believed this until one day I was traveling home to Ohio with all four of them. They were all under six years of age. An older gentleman was observing the five of us during a layover. He seemed very wise. We struck up a conversation, and I shared my funny joke with him. A peculiar grin began to develop on his face as he looked me straight in the eyes and began to laugh. "Oh no, no, no, the joke is on you...they are gonna *love* Daddy!" Now this took a moment to register, but when it did it was like the air slowly seeping out of a balloon. I had heard about mother-daughter relationships and how they can be rocky times.

Needless to say, I stopped laughing at Clint.

I often say that I don't think I did anything different in carrying and delivering, but our four daughters are all wired so differently! They have, and have always, had four very different personalities.

Our first, Hailey, from a young age has always been quiet. In pictures and videos she is always silently observing things. I would often wonder what she was processing in her little mind with her big, beautiful, dark round eyes full of wonder. She has been this way until recently when she has finally come out of her shell, and I can't wait to see how she continues to grow and evolve in this world and her beauty as a person.

Our second Leila is *very* boisterous. Damn that girl could scream; it was horrible! We nicknamed her "The Pterodactyl." Quite the personality, she has her own style and started dressing herself at three. She could hold a conversation with an adult at a very young age. It happened all the time, and people would look at me in disbelief after talking to her. By her second birthday, you could throw her in the middle of the deep end of a pool by herself and she would float to the top and make her way to the side of the pool. Again, she was two!

Sophia, the third, always seems to be up to something. She gets this very peculiar smile on her face and I look in her little eyes and wonder what she's scheming. But she was, and is, hilarious and loves to dance and sing...and guide her little sister around. Her and Sloan, the fourth, are attached at the hip. And no one is going to mess with Sloan. One time we were in a huge crowd and Sloan dropped her balloon. Some child picked it up. Sophia pushed through the crowd and made a bee line to the child and told her that the balloon was her sister's, as she gently took it out of her hand.

Sloan's always been the easiest child on the planet! I think maybe from being the fourth, she just had to be along for the ride. She never put up a fuss about anything, and when it came to Sophia, monkey see monkey do. She would just follow along with her. Sloan is still so sweet and has her dad's sense of humor; the things that come out of her mouth are hilarious. She loves her sisters very much and will go above and beyond to keep the peace in the house. She is so thoughtful. For Christmas once, she gave me a jar filled with sixty small pieces of paper, a loving comment on each one about all the things I have done for her (like give her life) as well as what she feels about me.

While they can all have their moments, all of them are sweet, caring, empathetic, sincere, loving humans. I don't know if this is how they came out and I am lucky, or if it had to do more with us as parents. Of course I would like to think the latter! Either way, Clint and I felt truly blessed.

In parenting, I saw even more of Clint's patience, humor, and empathy. Simply put, he was an amazing father, not just in how he handled the four girls, but me as well.

I called him crying one night when Hailey was five. I cannot remember the reason, but she said "I hate you!" I was devastated. How could my sweet baby say that to me? I called him, he listened, and replied, "Mommy, do you really think a five-year-old knows what the word 'hate' means?" Another time I had hidden their Easter baskets underneath a big blanket in my closet. I walked in, and Hailey was looking underneath it. I about lost it on the poor girl! All I could think was I had ruined the magic of the Easter Bunny! Clint's reply was "Mommy, children have the attention span of squirrels. Cover it back up, and she won't remember in the morning." I would go to him about stories of kids being kidnapped, the stories I could make up in my mind, the fear of something happening to my kids, whatever you can imagine. He'd reply, "Think about how many people are on this planet. Now think about how many crazy people are on this planet. I am surprised it doesn't happen more." That's all it took, and I would feel relieved.

I had the man of my dreams. I had the family I always wanted. I had my ideal life.

Of course, nothing is *ever* perfect, and I had things I had to continue to fight. The eating disorder had become such a part of me I couldn't imagine it any other way. It was so multifaceted and complicated, I just accepted it. It had come and gone in some ways over the years, but whenever I needed a sense of control, I went back to it. As a parent, I often fought with that need for control in my life. Control made me feel strong, it gave me something I could be proud of and got me noticed. Once I found that control and saw how I benefited from it, now I had to keep it and the feeling that being thin gave me. This went on for years, and soon it was just as much a part of me as my body is a part of me...at least that is what I thought. Soon it turned into controlling the sadness that would come, but it brought more sadness and everything just kept spinning.

There were no drugs at this time. As I approached marriage and motherhood, I had been already clean for some time. That depression that came with coming down, and my focus on being the best wife and mother I could be, kept me away. The fear of that depression and addiction ultimately saved me, even as I struggled with the occasional thought of how the drugs used to help me control my eating habits...

Clint had his issues as well. He worked in the casinos, and he was a people pleaser. Everyone wanted to hang with the guy, as he was just so much fun to be around. Also he could get everyone in to the clubs and restaurants, and everyone coming to Vegas wanted to party. It never occurred to visitors that the people who live there actually are *not* there to party but have to work and go home to families. Clint would always be hit up for things. So he would get friends, family, and colleagues in to places and most of the time they would coax him into hanging out for a drink... which often became a few drinks. Many nights I would lie awake at home wondering when he would be home. The way my brain works, I always assumed the worst, that something horrible was going to happen. I would be very worried in the wee hours of the morning when he still wasn't home. Every time. There has always been something about hard alcohol that strikes a nerve in me, something I'm sure comes from the memory of my father always having a glass with something. Beer and wine was totally fine, but the minute I saw Clint with a hard cocktail, my energy shifted and I felt nervous and angry. Now before that sounds too crazy, Clint had proven time and time again that he couldn't just stop after a couple in order to keep his composure. It scared me to see him after he drank too much. He was my protector, and alcohol took that from me. I didn't understand why anyone would need to drink that much. I knew my reasoning for indulging to extremes, so I wondered if he was trying to numb something inside him? I loved him so much, but this was the one thing that could possibly tear us apart. This was where my fear of loss of control would creep in.

But we did what all loving couples do and we talked about it and tried our best to handle it. The same was true with my eating disorder, though to be completely honest, I never fully revealed the extent of it when we were together. I had kind of let Clint in on it when we were in Chicago. There were many times where it tumbled out of control, especially in the early stages of our life together. I kind of opened up to see a reaction in Clint but even then didn't completely give it away. I somehow managed to put a lighter spin on it. I remember waking up the next morning, and he had left for work leaving a bunch of articles of things he had looked up for me to read.

This is actually a regret I have. For as amazing as our relationship was and always will be, this was the one thing I never really opened up about to Clint. What pains me is that with some reflection (and a lot of therapy), I know Clint would have still accepted me and would have done whatever I needed to help me deal with it. I was so embarrassed that I had to hide my issue from the one person who loved me for me. He could have been, in many ways, a guide or at least my rock on the path to letting this issue go. I do regret not sharing more with him as he had proven to be the ultimate partner.

In our final months, weeks, and days together, that partnership proved to more invaluable than anything.

It's still what I miss the most.

CHAPTER 23
MY VISION BOARD

It had been eighteen years since I first arrived in Las Vegas. It was 2009 and my youngest was seven months old. We had a family of four and were looking for a change.

Clint was hired to work for a large restaurant group in L.A. Making the move took some serious conversations. Vegas was his town. He went to UNLV, had made many relationships in the restaurant and hotel business, and had amazing friendships with colleagues and co-workers. This was a tough decision. Should we chance something like this? After all, despite the chaos of Vegas, we were comfortable. L.A. would be

a whole other ballgame. It would be different since I had been there last and now I had a rock by my side to help me avoid all the bullshit that comes with L.A. Life is about taking chances. Still, with Clint, four kids, and a dog, the stakes would be a little higher!

Time for an aside...in 2005, I was inspired to put together a vision board that I could put out to the universe and perhaps help manifest. I loved practicing yoga, so I put pictures of yoga and words that symbolized yoga. I wanted four children, though I had two at the time, so I put a picture of four kids roasting marshmallows over a fire. And deep down, more than anything, I wanted to live in a little beach town where my kids and I could walk everywhere and enjoy the weather and the community. I originally got this idea when I first met Clint and he brought me to Coronado Island where his family vacationed every summer. I had never been anywhere like it. I longed to live in a sweet little town like that, like something out of a fairy tale. I put pictures of us as a family on Coronado Island from when we visited that summer.

Four years later, we now had four children, and we were loading up the truck and moving to Manhattan Beach. Clint just happened to stumble upon the community while in L.A. for business and it was everything we both wanted. We rented a sweet little house up on a hill two blocks from the beach. It had a huge picture window with bench seats with the most beautiful unobstructed view of the ocean. I still live there today, and I am still pinching myself.

Oh, and I started practicing and teaching yoga. How that happened is still amazing to me. When I started practicing, I used to look at the instructor and think there was no way I could get up there and

lead a group of people. I don't know what it is, but I could dance in front of thousands and feel so comfortable, but speaking even to a small group of people scared the hell out of me. Still does. Nevertheless, yoga brought a sense of calm to me that I had never experienced before, and I wanted to do more with it. Clint saw it too, especially how much it benefited me. I decided to take the training course to become an instructor, even though it was fairly expensive. In his typical Clint sense of humor, he recommended that I take two! Not long after, I was a yoga instructor.

My vision board came true.

Still, it wasn't easy, and now that I had all I wanted, I was constantly in fear of losing it all. Sure enough, nine months after we arrived, the economy crashed and Clint lost his job. We had been so lucky to find this house. However the rent was double our mortgage payment of our huge house in Vegas, and now we didn't know how we were going to afford it. I was crushed. Where are we going to go? We couldn't afford to stay there.

There are angels in this world.

We told our property manager what had happened as we decided to start looking for a place inland to move. After checking out one place with all the kids, we got back in the car and were pulling out of the driveway. Clint's cell rang. It was the property manager. When the call was done, he looked at me and said, "The owners sympathize with our circumstance and they are willing to bring the rent down until we can get back on our feet."

Who does that? We had never even met them. I was blown away that they would do this for us, and feeling even more grateful that we were going to be able to stay.

That solved one of the problems. Now Clint had to find a job.

Deep down Clint had always wanted to open his own restaurant. We used to watch the television series *Restaurant Nightmares*. Honestly that was all I needed to confirm my feelings about never wanting to have *anything* to do with any restaurant. Not Clint though, he was determined.

During our Coronado Island trips we frequented a place called Cafe 1134. It was the cutest little restaurant. It had a laid back, comfy, cozy vibe and served amazing food, especially breakfast. He thought that if he could pull something like that off in Manhattan Beach, that would be pretty special. There was a building that had been vacant for quite some time. It was a pretty sad little building actually, right on the main street that goes through the town. It was brown on the outside, and with only two small windows, the inside was very dark. While the wheels started turning in Clint's mind, the anxiety was building in mine. But who was I to crush his dream? He quickly--though nervously--signed an eighteen-year lease!

Restaurant Nightmare would be ours.

Clint brought in his friend Chris who knew construction (Clint didn't!) to help renovate the spot. We had just put a huge chunk of money down. We had zero money coming in. Although we were on a tight budget, there was still money going out. We had no insurance, and we were a family of six renting a home in Manhattan Beach. The math didn't add up well for us.

The re-construction began. My job was to supply the peanut butter and jelly sandwiches every day at lunch for the crew... seriously. Oh, the *entire* crew consisted of Clint and Chris! And really, if we're being honest, it was just Chris. Clint was definitely a visionary, but a carpenter, engineer, or even run-of-the-mill construction worker, he was not!

This took about three months and during this time, Clint befriended quite a few locals. Between his funny demeanor and the fact that he was a big friendly teddy bear, he fit right in. He wanted the restaurant to look done enough as possible by December, for the Holiday Stroll, an event that takes place every year in the north end of Manhattan Beach. Although you could only see about a third of the restaurant that was done, it looked really good. There were now big windows, and the ceiling was open with exposed beams. It was bright, cheery, and had a comfy, laid-back vibe...just like he had wanted.

Contrary to my fears, it looked like the place was coming together.

On January 19, 2010, Four Daughters Kitchen opened its doors to a very welcoming community that was ready for something new.

Despite how much I *hated* the restaurant business and vowed never to have anything to do with it again after my Cheesecake Factory serving experience, I actually did help with 4DK. Granted, it only happened a few *years* after it opened, but still. I don't know what got into me, but I woke up one day and told Clint I wanted to wait tables. He was ecstatic, finally believing that I was coming on board with  this crazy idea. I told him not to get too excited; the only reason I wanted to do it was to get over the fear of it and prove to myself I could have a better experience the second time around. So for six months, while the girls were in school, I worked there...and I kicked butt! I know it seems so silly, but it was so empowering for me because I had built up such fear around it. Again, determination has never been a problem with me.

Now that the restaurant was open, the hunt was on for Clint to find a job. We knew it would be quite a while before the restaurant would bring in any money, and that was *if* it could even survive the first year. He was hired on as the director of restaurants at the Cosmopolitan, a new hotel scheduled to open in Las Vegas.

The irony, right? Clint was going to have to go back to Vegas. This was not an easy decision. The last thing we wanted to do was split up, but it was such a dream come true to be living here, we wanted to try our best to see if we could sustain it. Clint handed over the keys to Chris to handle the day-to-day operations. He handed me the responsibility of the day-to-day operations of raising four girls. For the next year he worked in Vegas. Even though he would try to visit us twice a month, we missed him.

I can't help but think that maybe the time that he was away in Las Vegas was meant to be sort of a practice for what was to come.

After the Cosmopolitan was up and running, he was hired to run a restaurant in Los Angeles. As an aside, the owner ironically was a heart surgeon. The universe can only do so much to send you signs. It's up to you to listen! Clint and I had always talked about when we turned forty years of age, that we would go get full physicals to make sure we were in tiptop shape.

Needless to say, forty came and went.

It was great having him back. For the next year he stayed put until another opportunity arose. Clint loved getting involved at the very beginning of a project. He loved helping to build concepts and putting together a rock-star team, as he would put it. This is what fueled him, this was his passion. So off he went on a few different restaurant adventures. He spent the next couple years doing this as we could not live on Four Daughters alone.

But eventually, he started to feel uneasy about all of it and the stress was taking its toll. There were many factors at play, but ultimately, he had enough and for his own sake, quit.

It was time to come home...for the last time.

For the next two months it was family time, beach volleyball, and his personal favorite, napping! That is if he could find a place in the house where he would be hidden from the girls, who always wondered where Daddy was. It was all of us connecting, enjoying each other and the life that we had built. It was a celebration of the Clausens and everything that made us...us. We didn't know it at the time, but it was us preparing our hearts for what was to come, to help us look past the stress, the chaos, the time away, and the dark times, and to remember all the love and light that we had embraced in our lives together.

We had Clint for two more months before disaster hit, and I consider that a gift from the universe.

CHAPTER 24
GONE

"Mommy, come sit on my lap for a minute." He called me Mommy and I called him Daddy ever since the girls were born. That's just something that two people who were in love and raised beautiful children together did. Or maybe they didn't. We didn't care. It's what we did, and it was one of a million ways we showed our love for each other.

Against my natural instincts to finish my task, something told me to listen. Thank God I did. I stopped what I was doing and went to join him. My sister, who was just as crazy as me, stopped what she was doing and came to join us as well. I stretched out across Clint's lap, enveloping myself in his arms one last time. As if controlled by something bigger than us, we were led to each other, to be with each other, heart-to-heart and connected at the end.

While I was sitting on his lap, he asked me if I was comfortable. He was holding me like a parent would hold their child. I was lying across his lap, my head resting on his arm. I told him I was, and a quick thought went through my mind about how sweet it was for him to ask. The very next moment, I felt him take a large inhale, his entire chest completely expanded. Then all I heard was a loud exhale, and suddenly...

Nothing.

Everything.

Nothing.

Of course, I thought he was joking. This was something Clint would do. I looked down at his arm hanging there, and he didn't move. I probably even laughed or at least smiled and that's hard to think about. Finally, I turned my body to see his face.

Nothing.

That's when I knew something was wrong. When we all knew. And the rest is chaos. Horrible chaos.

I yelled his name.

Again, nothing.

Then I looked at Jason with a questioning look. My brother, realizing something was seriously wrong, jumped up, grabbed his body, and pulled him to the floor. We thought he was maybe having a seizure because just then his body began to convulse. My brother held him down. Then Clint vomited, so Jason quickly pushed him on his side.

Upstairs, my brother-in-law Matt had just climbed into bed, letting out a sigh of relief as we had avoided any accidents or incidents on this family reunion trip to South Carolina. Between all the kids, the boat, the ocean, the pool, there was so much that could go wrong. Just as he was finally allowing himself to get comfortable, he heard his wife scream for him at the top of her lungs.

"MATT!"

The house was big and had a huge wide winding staircase. Matt was fast, but the kids were faster. All the kids (minus Leila, who was adjacent to the room we were in) came running down the stairs ahead of him. Kelly saw them coming and instantly ran to the bottom of the staircase and yelled at them to stop, turn around, and go back upstairs. Just then Leila screamed, "Daddy!" My sister ran back, swooped Leila up and took her upstairs to be with the other kids. By this point, Matt had come bolting into the room, and he and Jason were trying to revive Clint. There was no hesitation in their actions and they worked as hard as they could while Kelly was on the phone with the 911 operator.

I did nothing. I couldn't. I was frozen. Numb. I had experienced an out-of-body experience before in both bad times and good, but never anything like this. My brain couldn't process what was happening, and I was physically stuck. There were no thoughts, no emotions, nothing. I simply stood there observing, completely shut down and in a state of total shock. Maybe I would have reacted differently if I had been alone with Clint and didn't have Jason, Matt, and Kelly there to act. I'll never know.

When I finally started to come to, at least somewhat, I stared at him and it registered. My husband was in serious trouble. As the room seemed to be spinning around me, I walked over to him. He was on the floor. I was standing right above him, and I stared straight down into his eyes. He stared straight back, but he was looking through me, not at me.

Why is he not looking at me?

Matt clapped his hands together very loudly, right in front of his face, breaking my gaze. "Come on Clint!"

This also started to break me out of my daze. Did he see something I didn't? I looked back down at Clint to see if he was moving, and I joined in with Matt.

"Come on Clint!"

Even in that quick glimpse of hope, I couldn't help but notice the sensation of loneliness that began to cover me, like syrup as it slowly oozes down the side of a stack of pancakes. I knew something was seriously wrong, but I think even in that moment, as we tried to revive Clint and waited for the paramedics, there was a small part of me that knew this was going to be the end.

All the kids were upstairs with Aunt Angel. They were sitting on the floor in a prayer circle. A child of the social media age, Hailey had posted "Please pray for my Daddy" and soon everyone back home knew that something was going on before we could take it down. The calls started coming in. Something that I would learn later has stuck with me over the years. Jade, my brother's daughter, was five at the time and was in the prayer circle. She looked at Angel, her mother, and suddenly said, "Mommy, Uncle Clint died" very calmly and in front of my daughters. Angel quickly hushed Jade, but later when she was tucking her into bed, she asked why she would say something like that.

"He's fine," Jade replied. "I saw him. He smiled and waved at me."

After a while, the paramedics arrived and did what they could to try to revive him. It was decided he needed to be taken to the hospital. I was told to get into the ambulance, which I did, and waited for what seemed like an eternity. It was as if someone had a remote and was controlling my every movement. Not knowing what else to do, I began calling his sisters and brothers. I couldn't call his mother. How in the world could I tell a mother something that devastating about their child? I couldn't reach anyone. I had tried to avoid calling his baby sister, Crystal, who was very pregnant, but when nobody else answered, I had no choice. She was the only one I could get through to.

I don't know if I explained things right. I'm sure I didn't. Crystal couldn't understand what I was saying and honestly, I have no idea what I was saying. I waited impatiently for them to load Clint into the ambulance so we could get to the hospital and get him the help he needed.

Did I think he was still alive? I don't know. All I knew was that I wanted him to be and that was keeping me going and believing. As he was being wheeled in, I told a very confused Crystal that I had to go. I looked back and could see the top of Clint's head. It was purple. It all felt so wrong.

"Is this normal?" I said to the driver with sheer panic in my voice. "Have you ever seen anyone come back from this?"

He stared straight ahead, sweat dripping down his temple.

"I'm sorry, ma'am, I cannot answer that question," he said uncomfortably. "You will have to ask the paramedics. They know what they are doing."

We both knew the real answer.

In the deepest, darkest reaches of my psyche, an even bigger question began to emerge: What was I going to do now?

I wouldn't allow it to slip into my conscious mind, but it was there. It had always been there since the day Clint and I first met and fell in love. My life had been a lost journey before him, and though I was still battling my demons and keeping secrets from him (to protect him, I told myself), he had been my guiding light. He was my pillar, my happiness, my hope. He was my love and my life. I had made so much progress in clawing my way out of the various traps the darkness had set for me over the years, and it was because he was there to lend me his strength and his smile. What would I do if he was gone? Not if...not any longer. It was a question I hoped and prayed I would never have to ask myself and yet, here and now, I could feel that question lurking in a place I had hoped was long since buried. It would soon come to the surface.

As we pulled out of the driveway and moved along the open roads to the hospital, I was snapped back into reality by my conscious mind that had questions of its own.

Why were we driving so slowly and why weren't the sirens on?

Remember the old television series *The Twilight Zone*? I would equate the evening spent at the hospital to a scene from that show. When we arrived, it must have been around 11 p.m. There was no one there besides the person working behind the desk and one female doctor. At least that is all I remember. Nobody was in the waiting room. Nobody was in the emergency room. Where were all the doctors, patients, family members, friends? I wondered if it was all a façade, if there was nothing on the other side of those menacing doors. After all, nothing else seemed real.

The hospital was very clean and not very big. It smelled new, which I realize was a weird observation for me to make. Straight in through the doors, there was a desk area. To the left was the area that they brought the people in to take them to triage. To the right was the waiting area with a few chairs. To the right of that was a door. I noticed that door right away and kept glancing at it.

I knew what that door was for, and as much as I didn't want to believe it, I knew at some point we would be entering through it.

Kelly, Jason, and my stepbrother Mike had followed the ambulance and joined me there. Eventually Matt arrived as well. He had been back at the house making sure all was in order before we left. There were people in the house because my mom had run out to flag down the ambulance, and the neighborhood had come in to see if everything was ok. There is something to be said about southern hospitality.

The time spent in the waiting room was perhaps the hardest part of the evening. It always is, isn't it? The waiting? My thoughts were everywhere and nowhere. I was both numb and completely sharp and aware of my surroundings. Yes, I felt everything and nothing.

And the waiting went on, and on, and on.

That time, everything was all so confusing. It seemed like forever before they wheeled him in, and I only saw that out of the corner of my eye. I had a difficult time answering the questions about my insurance, social security number, etc. My mind could not focus on anything else but the shock of it all.

And we waited, and waited, and waited...

As time went by, I couldn't take it anymore. There were no answers, no information, nothing. Only questions that were now becoming too unbearable to leave unanswered.

"I want to see him."

I whispered it as we sat, stood, paced in total silence, each of us wondering what was happening.

I really felt like a pinball, just bouncing off the walls. Jason started yelling at the poor girl behind the desk, who also seemed a little clueless as to the hospital protocol. No one was giving her information so she couldn't give it to us. He was angry and demanded they let me back to see him. Kelly was by my side, in shock as well, but making sure she was there in any moment that I may need her. The longer we waited, the more those last images of Clint burned into my brain...as did the reality of it all.

Is this real? This can't be real. This is not the way this is going to go. But you saw his eyes, you saw the emptiness. He wasn't there. You know he is gone, but he can't be. No fucking way. I can't do this alone. This was not in the plan, no way. They should have let you go back by now. Someone would have come out and said something to you. Where are they? Where is he? You know he is gone. No he is not. Yes he is. You know what this feeling is.

Nothing.

Finally, the doctor entered the room. She was thin with dark hair. My sister Kelly said later she had no bedside manner. She did not like how the doctor handled the situation at all. I could tell in an instant by her body language it wasn't going to be good. She caught my eye from across the room and began to walk toward the door.

Why the fuck are you going to make this harder by making me go into that small room? Just fucking say it!

I don't remember if there was a label on the outside of the door. I don't even know what you would call the room if there was one. There was nobody but us in the waiting room. This move to this other room, behind those dreadful doors, was simply unnecessary. I just wanted it over with. The walk to and through that door was excruciatingly painful. I wanted to keep my distance. Once I was in that room, there was no going back.

She grabbed the handle, opened the door, and gestured for us all to go in. Everyone waited for me to move first, then they followed. I am very aware of the way I looked at her. It was a mean stare. I walked right by her and didn't take my eyes off of her, almost like this was her fault. I think there were a few chairs inside the very bland room. We all walked in, and she followed. I turned around. I was straight across from her with everyone else to my left. She leaned against the wall, shrugged her shoulders, put her arms up in the air, palms facing up.

"I don't know."

That's all this doctor had for me.

She kept gesturing with her arms and hands. "I don't know what to tell you. We don't know what it is or how it happened."

She never actually said Clint was gone. But I knew. We knew. Upon hearing the news, I flopped down on the chair behind me. I went limp and let out a painful sound from the deepest part of my gut. The finality of it all was simply too much.

After a few moments I sat up and looked at my sister, possibly so she could tell me it wasn't true. Her face was so soothing, and yet, full of truth. This was really happening.

Clint. Daddy. My protector. My confidant. My lover. My friend. My everything.

Gone.

I don't remember getting from that room to where Clint was so I could see him. Suddenly, I was just there. As I peered through the curtain, there he was, and this is the image that stayed with me during those first few weeks when I couldn't remember him or any moments with him. He had a neck brace on, his mouth was open, and he still had the tube they had put down his throat. His eyes were open.

Why wouldn't they have taken that stuff out or off before letting me see him?

My family all tried to give me some time with him, but I remember them close by. I touched Clint, and all I felt was the coldness of his body. I must have said something because I heard my brother demanding a blanket. I don't think the people that were there moved fast enough because Jason grabbed a sheet from somewhere and brought it in. My sweet brother...

I tried maneuvering myself so I could lie next to him on his left side, like I had done thousands of times before when he was alive. I needed to do that one last time. I took his arm and put it around me. I tried to hold it there, but that killed the fantasy. I needed it to stay without me making it stay. I put my head on his chest.

Wait a minute, what was that...I hear him breathing!

I lifted my head to look at his face, then listened.

There it is again! Should I call them? I hear something. Oh my god, maybe he is alive and in a coma! Maybe this can still all turn out ok!

I soon realized that the tube down his throat would fill with air as I lifted my head up and then the air would be pushed out of the tube as I laid my head on his chest. It sounded like he was breathing. He wasn't. It was time for me to start accepting what was happening here.

I kept telling him how much I loved him. Then I replayed things in my mind and started apologizing for stupid things. I am sorry I did this, I am sorry I did that. I apologized for things that he knew and things that he didn't. Our all too short time together came in flashes and it was fucking horrible to know that there would be nothing more to add to the wonders we had already shared together. I just tried to be with him, but I was lost, not even with myself.

How do you say goodbye like this?

Especially to the person that saved you.

You can't.

For some reason, I was worried that they wouldn't give me his things. I wanted his ring. I asked Matt to help me get it off. I am sure they would have returned it later, but I didn't want them to take it. It wasn't easy, but he got it off.

I then thought I needed to call his sisters and brother. They needed to say goodbye to him while I was with him. This mattered. I talked to his brother Darren and asked him if I should try to reach everyone else to say goodbye. He calmly answered, "Kori, go back to your girls."

Yes, the girls. My girls. Our girls.

The back and forth began. If I leave, this is it. I was trying to take him in as much as I could. It was so hard to leave to say that final goodbye. But the thought of the girls got me going. That and realizing that those arms of his were not going to hold me as much as I tried to make them. He was not in that body anymore. I had to go where I was needed.

I got up and walked to the curtain, turning to look at him one more time. I then told everyone it was time to go. As we were leaving, I noticed that the sweatshirt my sister had given me off her back to wear on the way to the hospital that night had Clint's blood on it. I still have that sweatshirt. I never washed it. I used to look at it a lot.

To be honest, I don't recall any part of the drive back that night. I don't even remember walking into the house. It was as if I appeared in the room where all four of my daughters were sleeping. It was late, and per my request, my mother had put them all in the master bedroom so we could all be together when I got back. I woke them up, and they were all pretty out of it. I had them all sit with me on the bed. I looked at all of them, dreading what I had to say. I didn't believe it or understand it, so how were they supposed to? In the end, I said the only thing that mattered.

"Your daddy loved you very much. He wanted me to tell you that."

I acted like he said it before he died. I acted like I had a conversation with him about them. I didn't know how else to do it. They asked if they could go see him, and I explained that they couldn't.

"Why?"

And that's when I told them he died. There were tears, confusion, pain. But they were so exhausted that not long after, they all laid back down and fell asleep. Sophia couldn't. We lay in bed, and she cried. I held her until she finally drifted off.

I could barely stay still, my whole body was buzzing. Even with all my family there, I suddenly felt so scared and alone. Sleep was not going to happen. I just wanted to go back to earlier that day. To go back in time. There had to be a way to change this situation. No, this was permanent. Never has a word resonated so deeply with me since that day. The night seemed to drag on forever.

Then I saw my sister walk past the windows of my room. She was outside on the huge deck that wrapped around the front of the house. She walked straight out and stopped, looking out at the water. I went to her and felt a moment of relief. That's where we stayed the rest of the night, sitting on a bench with my head on her lap and her grazing her fingers through my hair. No words were spoken.

Not one.
Nothing.

CHAPTER 25
THERE IS ALWAYS
THE NEXT DAY

There is always the next day.

Whether you want it to come or not, it arrives and with it, especially after a tragedy, comes the process of healing, rebuilding, moving on, living. They say life goes on. For me, that reality hit the very next day.

As horribly painful as it is.

As I watched the sun rise, closing the book on the worst night of my life, I waited patiently for the girls to wake up. The pain I was feeling had to be written all over my face. I told them a second time that their daddy was gone. They heard, but I wasn't sure they understood, especially the little ones.

They once again asked if they could go and see him. All of a sudden I was consumed with guilt.

Why didn't I have them come to the hospital last night? They could have said goodbye to him. I could have made that decision. How unfair was it that I was able to say goodbye, but I took that away from them?

This was the first big decision I had made on my own...and in my mind, I had failed. Clint was always the one who made the big decisions, at least that's what I thought. He was the one I could rely on to look at all sides, to think about things calmly and rationally, to make the big call. From now on, I was going to have to do all of that on my own. I felt so lost and scared. I was already messing this up. How was I possibly going to survive as a widowed, single parent?

Oh my god.

I was a widow and a single parent.

As exhausted and hurt as we all were, we needed to deal with some logistics from the trip. The original plan was to fly home at nine in the morning and that obviously wasn't happening. Everyone began going about their normal business, just literally going through the motions. We all had to pack up our things and vacate the house so it could be cleaned and ready for the next group. I felt like a mouse in a maze, wandering around aimlessly. I just couldn't grasp the fact that we had to leave without him. I kept thinking how Clint was here with us less than twenty-four hours ago. Just yesterday, we were all in the back watching him play softball with the kids.

That was *yesterday!*

Packing Clint's things was the worst part. I tried to get through it as quickly as possible. That would be my habit for quite some time, when it came to things dealing with Clint's passing. Do what you need to do to get through it and do it quickly.

That's not always the best way.

We packed up the cars and headed back to Kelly's house. The silence was so clear. Everyone was consumed by the shock and dealing with it silently in their own way. I mean, what do you say? What do you talk about? Like a bunch of zombies, we were mindlessly going through the motions of the day.

Again, decisions had to be made, and unfortunately I had to be the one to make them. How could I be qualified to do this? I wasn't. But I quickly realized there was no more room for that scared little girl anymore. In the next two days that followed I quickly became an expert at dealing with the logistics. Dealing with the pain, loss, guilt, and everything else would be a different story. But that would come later. Now, I had distraction.

I had to plan how to move forward.

The next couple of days were spent finishing up the details, deciding when we should head back home, and how we were going to celebrate Clint. Along with the buzzing and vibrating sensations in my body, my heart literally felt as hard as a rock. My tear ducts were completely dry by this point. As much as I wanted to still cry, I could not muster up one tear.

How can you when you don't feel anything?

I floated from room to room wondering what was going on in everyone else's mind and trying to block out what was going on in mine. If I'm being honest, it would be a long time before I would completely let those thoughts in. Even in the days immediately following Clint's death, we still took the girls to get their hair cut and to shop for the dress I would wear to a pending wedding. It was my first realization that even in the depths of tragedy, time moves forward, as my sister Kelly said.

It was Saturday when we left Isle of Palms and went to Kelly's house, and that Tuesday we headed home.

What's amazing is that minus the obvious, that was one of the best trips any of us had ever been on. Even the girls, when they went back to school, talked about how awesome of a time they had. I couldn't believe how differently they saw everything. Leila, just three weeks after she lost her father, got up in front of her class to talk about her amazing trip to South Carolina. When she was done speaking, a boy raised his hand and asked innocently, "Didn't your dad die while you were there?" Leila simple answered, "Yes he did." The teacher pulled me aside later that day. She was amazed at how Leila handled it. To this day, it is still their favorite trip they talk about. It was full of love and laughter and fun and connecting with those who mattered most. Unbelievably, the trip was never marred by the tragedy we all endured at the end. It remains a source of light in our lives.

That says something.

And if we really look at it, perhaps that trip happened to prepare us for the inevitable. Perhaps it had to happen there and then because we were surrounded by love and had the strength we needed to endure.

I've come to find comfort in that.

As we were leaving, I remembered that we didn't have seat assignments on the flight. While we waited at the gate, I wanted to make sure that the girls and I were all sitting in the same general vicinity on the plane. When I asked about this, the way the flight attendant reacted, you would have thought I spilled coffee all over her desk. There went that numb buzzing again. Where was my protector? He would have said something to make me laugh.

We sat in one long row; three seats, then the aisle, then three seats. One of those seats was empty. It was always going to be empty. I couldn't stop staring at it, knowing who was supposed to be there. At one point during the flight, the turbulence was becoming quite noticeable. I looked over at all the girls, concerned about them. They were sound asleep, emotionally exhausted, I'm sure. As I clenched the armrests, one thought passed through my mind.

Go ahead, take us down. Then we can all be together.

Then a slight smile grabbed the corners of my mouth. I think it was the first time I had smiled since Clint had passed. And all it took was a morbid joke? Thought? Wish?

We arrived back in L.A. I knew that the next obstacle to get over would be walking through the front door of our home. The dream home. The one we had built together as a family. The one that would now feel just a bit emptier. No, not a bit. There would be a huge hole. A Clint-sized hole.

We stood outside our home in a huddle. We had our arms

wrapped around each other, the pain welling up in our hearts. The sound of loud sobbing tears rang out into the air. For a while, we simply couldn't move. Finally, when we were ready, we walked in, and yes, emptiness encompassed the room.

My heart would not feel, and my mind could not remember. I tried so hard to conjure an image of anything other than him lying in the hospital bed that night. That picture of him was so embedded in my brain and nothing else could penetrate. I would go back to the guilt I felt for not bringing the girls to see him that night. I now know I did the right thing, but then I was filled with regret.

We did what we could. We unpacked, and tried to settle in to the comfort of a now changed home. I was so desperate for him to hold me, I went into his very small closet and snuggled myself in his laundry that was on the floor in a pile. It was a bunch of his nice work suits and shirts that still smelled like him. It was comforting and awful at the same time as I knew eventually, even that smell would fade.

Over the next several days, I wandered up and down the streets around my home, just watching and listening. There was music playing, people laughing, kids running around. How could they be having fun? They seemed so happy, I just couldn't understand this. My whole world had just come crashing down. The thought of ever feeling that happiness again seemed impossible.

Luckily we did have friends and they were all waiting at home with open arms. In months to come I would hear the stories of where they were when they heard the news. As it turned out, a group of them happened to be eating at Four Daughters Kitchen. They saw my daughter's social media post. The news quickly spread. Being together in shock was better than being alone.

In the weeks to come we did everything we could to celebrate Clint's life. The first celebration would be the paddle out, which as I mentioned in my introduction, was the most beautiful thing I had ever experienced. The outpouring of love was amazing.

Besides the paddle out, we had a huge Celebration of Life which was held at the home of Clint's best friend in Las Vegas, where we had celebrated our wedding reception. Clint had opened and worked in quite a few restaurants in Las Vegas. Needless to say many amazing chefs and colleagues helped put together an event that I know Clint would have loved!

But the first of the gatherings would be the wedding of his baby sister Crystal. I always felt sad about this. Her wedding date just happened to be the weekend after he passed. There was talk of postponing it, but Clint wouldn't have wanted that. Besides, we all needed to be together. I feel like she got a bad deal. Clint was always the life of the party, so when a wedding rolled around, everyone would patiently await his infamous speech. That evening, the elephant in the room was hard to ignore. God bless Crystal, she held her own that night. I will always be proud of her and her strength.

In the weeks, months, and even years to come, I wished that I had that strength.

Eventually, all too soon, the celebrations and gatherings came to an end. People had to get back to their own lives. We had to try and settle into ours.

And I needed to seek answers.

Clint died of a massive heart attack due to an enlarged heart. The exact term is "severe coronary artery atherosclerosis." When he died, two of his arteries were almost completely clogged. What's worse is that it wasn't noticed. At Clint's last physical, he was given the all clear. He had even had an EKG done the year prior and nothing popped up. Nobody knew anything was going to happen.

The day after Clint passed, I was sitting on the steps talking to the pathologist about the autopsy. He needed to know if Clint was taking any medications or supplements. As far as I knew the only thing he had been taking was his inhaler. He had been using it more and more over the years as his exercise-induced asthma seemed to be getting worse and worse.

After arriving back home, the work began on retrieving passcodes for bills, accounts, emails, etc. Unfortunately we had not set ourselves up in the event something should happen to one of us. Chad, a close friend of the family, stepped in to help me with this. He was even able to open Clint's phone. I loved seeing his pictures and reading his funny texts.

Unfortunately I also began reading some text chains that had to do with him not feeling well and his energy being very low. It looked as though human growth hormone was recommended from his trainer. He mentioned that shipments from Mexico were available for purchase. Although I am not sure how long he had been taking this, I do remember him feeling really good and having great energy. In reading the texts, it looked as though he was without it for a bit. Clint seemed anxious because he wasn't feeling well.

I of course did some research on this and did see the side effects that can occur and what the ramifications were. I didn't like what I read, but I felt worse about not knowing that he was feeling bad and needing to take something. We probably could have made better choices with someone who could give more knowledgeable advice. I don't place blame. Lord knows I took a lot of things for less legit reasons. Still, I wish I had known and that we had explored options together. I wish he had talked to me about it. I wish I had been more observant. I wish, I wish, I wish.

Wishing things were different was how I would spend my time for quite a while. I could even argue, at times, even today. Wishing...

...and escaping.

Sometimes in the worst possible ways.

I have been trying and working to recover from *that* more than anything else as I look forward.

CHAPTER 26
THE CHOICE TO LIVE

I don't want to write these next few chapters.

Even now, even after I've learned how good it is to get these things out there, to acknowledge them so I can move past them, I struggle with this. It is embarrassing, painful, shameful, and... human.

I tried my best. Ok, I know that's not true, but I did what I felt I had to do. I was lost and unsure of how to cope so I found peace, comfort, strength, and solace, no matter how fleeting, anywhere and everywhere I could. Even reverting back to some of those familiar demons. I simply tried to survive, and in doing so, I caused harm. To me, my family, my girls, and the memory of a man who meant everything. Yes, I am hard on myself, and you'll soon see why. Perhaps you'll judge me as I have. Perhaps you'll understand and sympathize, at least partially, as I'm coming to do. Perhaps, this will all seem familiar.

We are complicated creatures, capable of great strength and tremendous weakness. Those points where we are at our highest and lowest are the ones that define our lives. Luckily, I've learned that regardless of where you're at, it's never too late to get yourself back to balanced. Even if it takes time.

Years.

The few years after Clint died, collectively, up until recently, equal the worst of my life. Yet, they may prove to be my salvation as they made me face who I was before, during, and after my relationship with Clint. Going down the rabbit hole eventually leads you to a place where you have to look at yourself, confront those demons, and make the hard choice.

The choice to live.

If not for yourself, then for those you love. Those who depend on you.

I have made that choice.

Finally.

I'd like to just write about that, about how I've grown and where I'm at now. I feel, if I'm allowed a moment of pride, that this is where I could possibly inspire, where I could help others dealing with tragedy. It's what I always wanted my story to be.

But I promised to be honest, however painful. That's part of this process, and there is still so much work to be done. I'm not there yet. Probably not even close. I still need to face these things. I need to remember. I need to shine light on the darkest years of my life.

To all those who were affected, especially my four beautiful daughters, I am so unbelievably sorry...

I was not always this open and honest. In fact, I still fight it. I've hinted at this before, but I need to say it (or write it, I guess). I had many secrets that I hid from Clint, and many others who loved me. From myself. The eating disorder, the drug abuse, the rape, the photographer, Cal...all of it, for most of my life, has been my own little secret. I was always so ashamed and afraid of anyone finding out. I was in fear that if they did, they would think of me the same way I thought of myself.

If I didn't love myself, why would anyone else?

This manifested into pressure, darkness, guilt, sadness, frustration, and rage once Clint was gone. Even though he didn't know about these things from my past, these things that still affected me, he was a rock that kept me tethered to a happier reality that we were building together. I cannot stress enough how much I regret keeping secrets from him. If I hadn't, we could have processed together. He would have understood. He loved me unconditionally. If I hadn't been so afraid, we could have both worked to help me get past these traumas and feelings of unworthiness. We could have built me up together. I would have been stronger and more prepared.

We didn't. And I wasn't. So I fell and fell hard into the darkness without him.

Funny enough, not long after Clint's passing, I met someone who was and still is a source of not only light in my life, but also, in many ways, my salvation. At the very least, through years of work, stress, tears, and confrontation, sometimes blurring the lines of professional and personal, this man helped me get to a place where I could save myself. To only call Kevin my therapist would not be giving him enough credit. He is a gift from the universe, one that I've sorely needed over the years, one who has watched and helped me through the struggle and made me face my secrets, faults, self-doubt, and prospects of the future I want to live.

To be clear, this is a different therapist named Kevin than the one I had as a child. It took time, but Kevin became my new voice of reason. He took over where Clint left off. The only difference was he helped me to bring all these things to the surface. He helped me to realize that all these things did not define me, nor did I need to be ashamed of them. This took a long time. Trust had to be built, and I needed to feel comfortable. One by one I began to let them go. This was so difficult. How do you change thirty-four years of a pattern? Thirty-four years of a lie made up and believed.

I met Kevin at the paddle out, where he played music, and we connected soon after. I felt comfortable (enough) with him

 and started seeing him regularly, even though he had never worked with a patient dealing with tragedy and grief, particularly at the level at which I was suffering. This started a long and complicated relationship where we both were feeling out the best way to handle what I was going through and getting me to a place to move on. Kevin would see me through all the bad times...the ones I'm realizing now I'm taking too long to get to, that I'm avoiding. Again, I'm sorry. I'll stop putting this off.

One of the first things Kevin said to me at our first session was, "Why are you being so hard on yourself?"

That would take years to answer, and I would have to go through a lot of shit to avoid answering it before I finally found the strength to do so...

In the initial days, week, and months after Clint's passing, I was constantly surrounded by family and friends. My mother came out for extended stays. Kelly was in constant contact, as were many, many friends from the Manhattan Beach community. The house was always busy, and I think I liked it that way. My sister remembers coming to visit me once and getting overwhelmed with the busyness. She told me there was never peace and quiet in thehouse. Everyone was concerned and wanting to help out in anyway they could.

But eventually, there are less eyes on you as everyone gets back to the business of their daily lives. Of course, they would all be there if I needed them, but as time went on, they were less and less active when it came to *watching*.

That's when I started to slip. I want to be clear. I blame *no one* but myself. Everyone was ready to help with anything I needed. I just had become so good at keeping secrets and hiding any and all indiscretions that they couldn't see it. On the surface, for the most part, it looked like I was coping, at least initially. That would soon change. Deep down, I was dying, and what made it worse was that I didn't care. I just wanted the pain to go away.

There was so much pain.

I sunk down to the old habits, eating just enough to sustain. I lost weight as the bulimia kicked back in. My controlling urge of "don't eat, don't feel" was at an all-time high. And I didn't want to feel anything. Not one thing. I believed this would keep me safe from the pain as long as I could do it. Despite all the work I had done to get past this in my time with Clint, it came roaring back with a vengeful ease. It wasn't until later that I realized that the eating or lack of eating really had nothing to do with it. You don't feel if you don't allow yourself to feel. Period. But during this time, just like before, if I ate something I would start to feel sadness and depression and I would miss Clint. So I would purge and that loneliness would go away, at least for a moment. Clint would go away.

That was terrifying in itself. I began to lose not only all feelings, but all memories of Clint! I was so on autopilot, I didn't even notice what was happening. My heart was cemented through, and my mind could not, would not visit any memories. I remember getting so angry.

Why the fuck can't I remember him?

It was terrifying, like maybe he was gone forever. I realize now I was purposely blocking him and our time together out of my mind. If I thought about him, I would get sad and lonely. Again, I didn't want to feel so I purged those memories from my brain. If I did think of him, it was only of the final days and moments, wondering obsessively if there was anything I could have done differently. If there was any way he could still be alive.

I felt like I was just floating from room to room wondering what I should be doing, just passing time, almost like waiting for it all to be over and for Clint to come back so we could get on with our life. He wasn't, and I couldn't accept it. Still, life had to carry forward. Things like getting signed up for soccer, school, paying bills...all the things that do not stop just because Clint died.

Life.

I stayed so busy, just doing, doing, doing. I never stopped. I went from one thing to the next. The first six months I had so many people always around, coming and going, so there was no time to just sit with things. That's fine. It was the last thing I wanted to do. Don't think, don't remember. Don't feel. I wondered if people thought I was a cold-hearted bitch because I didn't cry.

In the evening, when things got quiet, I took Ambien, more than I should, trying to knock myself out before the weight of it all kicked in. I actually got to the point where I enjoyed just completely checking out. I started to look forward to it. I would get through the day as much as possible looking like I was handling everything like a pro and then embrace the relief as I checked out.

Physically, as time went on, I just felt exhausted. So much of that exhaustion was brought on by the energy it took to fake surviving. My generous friends were doing all kinds of things for us, but I never wanted to be a burden so I wanted to convince them that I was fine; I was strong; and I could handle whatever came my way. Yep, I was right back to "Fake it 'til you make it."

When I did finally want to cry, I introduced alcohol into my life once again.

A lot of alcohol.

This was perfect for me. It was a total depressant, and it allowed for at least some moments of relief, although short-lived. Alcohol soon became the crutch I needed to get by, and was a big contributor to my spiraling out of control.

Spiritually I don't remember feeling anything. That was unusual for me. I was almost trying too hard to look for signs. I wanted something concrete, like actually seeing Clint and hearing him tell me everything was going to be ok. I now realize that the true signs were very subtle and went unnoticed the more I kept my mind busy. I felt that Clint was nowhere near me. I was way too closed off to feel any sort of presence and this only added to the darkness.

Instead of feeling and celebrating him and easing into my life with the family I did have left, especially my strong and amazing daughters, I just let the anger surround me, even if I wasn't conscious of it. I was feeling tremendous anger about the shit that kept piling on during the first three and a half years after Clint passed. A lot of this had to do with the fact that I had to take over a restaurant I didn't want...but more on that later.

I still deal with that anger. I never wanted to act like a victim so I would tell myself to suck it up and move on...which I totally did! But I was actually experiencing anger that was growing into a rage. Then I felt angry that I couldn't seem to move on. The more time that went on I would tell myself, "Well it's been a year, it's been two years, it's been three years...you should be over this. No one wants to hear how much you miss him." I realize now by not feeling sad and by pushing the anger I felt, I actually did more harm than good. I even got mad at Clint for the mess he left for me to clean up.

In fact, in one session with Kevin, I actually said the words "Clint made it out easy!"

I believed it.

There was not much clarity in this time, but there were moments when reality set in.

I drank a lot during the first six months. My mother was staying with us and I could just disappear easily, which I did often. But this particular time she was not in town. I cannot remember who was with the kids. I was in Hermosa Beach and was supposed to go to my yoga studio's Christmas party. I ended up going out and having a drink or two first. I was just sitting by myself at a bar watching and listening to everyone. The effects of the alcohol kicked in quick because I also wasn't eating. I started crying but still decided to go to the party. I was crying so hard, I am assuming by the look on my friend's face when I walked in, that I did not look good. I left the party and called Kevin. I remember him being very concerned. He happened to be at his office and wanted me to come in, but I was too drunk to find it. He calmed me down and somehow got me home. I was standing in the living room, in complete darkness. I popped two Ambien, on an empty stomach and way too many drinks. I woke up on the floor after a few hours had passed. I opened my eyes. The living room was dark, and I stared at the ceiling. It was at this very moment that I realized that Clint was not there to pick me up and take me to bed.

I was alone.

This was it. I was right back to where I was when I was a little girl looking for the stability of a family life, to where I was when I was a teenager looking for the stability of love, to where I was as an adult looking for...for...what the fuck was I looking for?

Oh my god, my girls are going to live my experience? They are all going to fall into the same traps and make the same bad decisions. They are completely fucked now because he's gone...and I can't help them. I am everything I never wanted to be.

It was during these experiences and these thoughts and this darkness that I met regularly with Kevin. Our relationship has always lived in the gray areas. There is a special intimacy there, purely on a platonic level, but one nonetheless. I pushed boundaries, and Kevin struggled mightily to keep them yet still be available to me. In many ways, I began to see Kevin as a replacement for Clint. I know that we talked probably too often and he was probably overly accessible to me. He was more focused on doing what *heals* versus doing what was *professional*. I know that he was confused as to how to handle me. In fact, he said he was often scared and thought about referring me to a more experienced colleague who was more practiced in dealing with grief. I know we formed a unique therapeutic relationship that seemed to border on co-dependency, one that brought up whole other sets of emotions for me, good and bad.

I also know, one hundred percent, that I could not have survived without him.

In putting together this book, Kevin shared some of his notes and observations with me, from the first time he met me up until more recently. It's hard to see and hear, especially knowing that all of it is completely true.

He observed I was always anxious and disgruntled, that I had feelings of abandonment.

That I had a loyalty to my daughters and no clue how to care for them or help them build a future.

That I wanted answers and only answers, answers he couldn't give. When he couldn't, I would lash out.

That I was always uncomfortable, moving with agitation and building tension in the room.

I was angry, always angry.

That I wanted to be strong but didn't want to be noticed. I hated the attention this had all brought on me.

That I couldn't cry, not at first. He noticed how I held everything in. When I did let go, I couldn't stop apologizing for being weak.

That I didn't want to be alone.

How I wondered when this would all be done, when I would be healed.

He began to see the physical changes in me and started wondering about an eating disorder, alcoholism, hyper sexuality, and drug use. He was afraid I wasn't being honest.

He could tell I was scared, and he was afraid I was going to hurt somebody or myself.

I pushed him to push those boundaries...and sometimes he did cross them, taking my calls late at night. Or when I was on the ledge and rather than talk me down, he asked me how I wanted my girls to remember me. I made him promise never to leave me, like I feared he would. They all did. He got me to open up about everything: the drug use, the eating disorder, the rape, the craving for stability, my anger, frustrations, fear, all of it.

It took time, but that was the beginning of my effort to pull myself out of this darkness, an effort that still continues to this day. I fear it'll never end. How could it? You don't kill the demons, you just try to keep them at bay, ignoring their piercing cries and getting comfortable with them, taking them along for the ride. There were other things that helped push me to a better place, but my long and drama-filled work with Kevin was the start of the climb, and for that I'll forever be grateful.

However, beyond my own feelings, my old addiction and my newfound alcohol and Ambien addiction, there were still plenty of other mistakes, problems, frustrations, and more I would have to deal with, especially when it came to other men, my daughters, an old obsession, that fucking restaurant, and...my breasts.

In the interest of opening up completely, let's tackle them one by one, shall we, and get through this together, hoping there's light at the end of this bleak, painful, and sometimes ridiculous tunnel.

First up, men in the post-Clint years.

God help me.

CHAPTER 27
I WAS SO LONELY

What is difficult for me here is the fact that I truly loved Clint and missed him so much...but if this were true then how in the world could I fall into the arms of another man?

The truth is, I was so lonely. I just wanted to be wrapped in the arms of someone who cared, just to feel protected again. I immediately went back to the feelings I had as a little girl when I would go to a home of a family that was complete. Mine was not complete anymore. Just like when I was a child, it was broken. I had what I wanted for a while, but now I was back to feeling I wasn't worthy of it, so I couldn't have it.

That stability was once again so out of reach, I craved anything that looked even slightly like it. I went from eighteen years of companionship to nothing...I craved just to be held. Everything is a feeling, an intuition, a vibration. I think I've always felt that way though I've only recently learned how to express it. At the time, I was attracting what I was thinking and feeling, and I was vibrating at a very low frequency. Sadness, fear, unworthiness, anger...that's what I was attracting. The first couple men felt like total scammers who prey on weakness. At least, it felt like they were preying on mine. I cringe when I think about them. There was a man in his late thirties who lived on the street behind us. He pretty much kept to himself. He was good looking and quiet. I befriended him, and we started going for walks and talking a lot. He said he knew about Clint, and that was where I always melted. The fact that someone knew him and what happened made me think they would for sure have my best interest at heart. We talked about him a lot, and I enjoyed being in his company. I started going to his place after the girls were a sleep. Drinking was involved, which isn't very good for obvious reasons. He was so nice. He would hold me, and we would talk. It felt so good even if it was fleeting.

I disappeared one evening when my sister was visiting, and she came looking for me. He had been drinking, and he was trying to get me to stay. She heard all of this and was pissed. When I went back to the house, she confronted me, and we got into a huge argument. Not only was she surprised, she was also shocked that I could even do something like this so soon. This was exactly one year after Clint passed. The guilt and shame I felt made me immediately get defensive. I started crying and I yelled, "I am so fucking lonely!"

She then backed off. But the feeling she had gotten from him was not good. Soon after, I saw other women going in and out of his home. He then wound up checking himself into a hospital because he was suicidal. I think he was an alcoholic as well. One night, two police trucks showed up. They asked questions about him and looked in his windows. Long story short, he moved shortly after, and I never found out what happened to him.

Another time, a good-looking man in his thirties showed up at 4DK. I was sitting at the bar and we began talking. Again, he was very nice, and he was interested in talking and listening to me. On the same note, he wouldn't give up much info about himself... besides the fact that he was a loaded New York businessman. He had plenty of stories about that. That should have been a red flag.

He rented a place close to the restaurant and came in a lot. Soon we began going for walks, and he started asking about getting involved in the restaurant. He was asking all kinds of questions about the numbers, the business. He had ideas, and I finally told him to write a proposal of whatever he was talking about to help the restaurant. He found the concept of writing a proposal difficult, which was interesting considering his supposed profession. I totally ignored the feeling in my gut. I went out with him a couple times. I never was comfortable. I really can't say what I was thinking. But it was how I was when I was younger, and I had reverted back to that. I just wanted to be noticed, to be loved.

Sure enough, I soon noticed what a player he was, and an alcoholic.

Again.

He kept coming around. I was always nice of course, but eventually my hairs would stand on end when he would walk through the door. I began looking at his Facebook page and noticed every picture was of himself...alone. That was weird. Also, his ONE friend on Facebook was a widow, and it wasn't me.

He eventually left Manhattan Beach but would reach out every now and then or just show up at the restaurant. The very last time he showed up, he had called and said he was in "close by Colorado" and was thinking about hopping on a flight to L.A. to come say hi. I told him I was busy, but he showed up where he knew I would be...and he would not leave. I had to tell him at least five times I wasn't interested in going for a walk or hanging out. To this day I still think the situation was quite bizarre. But this was what I was attracting.

About six months later I met another man who I'll call Jonathan. I had heard a lot about him, and mutual friends were always saying I should meet him. I knew we had one thing in common; we both had lost a spouse. I considered that positive because we would understand each other. But that was all I really thought about. In fact, I didn't pay any attention to it until one day my friend called me up and said Jonathan had hurt his back and needed a massage. I agreed to it. He came to the house.

He was quiet and very matter of fact. I gave him the massage, and when he left I thought, "This is who they want to set me up with?" He was the polar opposite of Clint. Again, nothing came of it. Then one day he showed up at my yoga class. I ended up calling him by the wrong name and that led him to think he didn't have much of a chance (understandably so). I know I called him Steve a couple times. Then one day I received the funniest text explaining that although he loved the name Steve, that wasn't actually his name. Besides being mortified at my own mistake, I thought the text was fricking hilarious!

We talked for a few months, and I learned he was a very good man. What was even more impressive to me was the fact that he was an amazing father. He had four adult children, two from his first marriage and two from his second wife. I would like to say I fell for him but I'm not sure. I was actively looking for a distraction, something to keep me from feeling the constant pain of losing Clint. I really don't know. But I did develop feelings of some kind for Jonathan.

In typical Kori fashion, once I fall for someone, I have a tendency to focus on their needs. Jonathan was no exception. At the time I would have done anything for him. He was in a great deal of pain from his own loss, and I felt the need to take care of him. In doing so, I had to remind myself constantly that I had lost someone as well. We dated for a year and a half and we did a lot of fun things together. He was very romantic.

But we were dealing with our grief and pain in our own ways. We had two different mindsets that neither of us can be blamed for...we were just coping, and he was clearly lost on how to move on. Unfortunately, I paid the price. He never came around my place much or wanted to hang out with my friends. I'd have to constantly make excuses for his absence. He would lie to his kids, who he wanted to protect more than anything, about spending time with me. I had to listen to him speaking to his kids while we were on our way up to Mammoth. I had to hear his reply when they asked him who he was going there with. "Just me and the dogs." We couldn't be seen by his kids; we couldn't take pictures together; we had to spend evenings in hotels.

All of this was still happening after a year and a half of dating. Unfortunately for me, he was unable to accept me because I wasn't his wife. I don't know what I expected. I knew Jonathan held her in the highest regard, as Clint did me. I was so afraid of losing him that I allowed for certain behaviors. Unfortunately these things turned me in the direction of not feeling worthy. I felt like I was a hidden secret, and it made me feel dirty. I don't blame him. As I've learned, coping with grief doesn't exactly bring out the best.

The final straw was that he essentially told me there was no way we were going to ever combine our families, even for just a holiday or an outing. This came to a head one day when the littles, my two youngest, and I were at his house. We always went over on Sunday because they loved to play with his two dogs. We could stay for the day while he cooked and got ready for his Sunday night family dinner. He was an amazing cook. I always got to see the amazing meals he prepared, but we were never allowed to stay for dinner. I watched him take an adorable picture of my girls (the littles) and the dogs, but as I continued to watch, he zoomed in and cropped out the littles.

That was it. I confronted him a few days later. He admitted it and said he felt bad and that I deserved to be treated better. He just couldn't do it. So that was that.

Again, I don't blame him for anything. He was coping the only way he knew how. Plus, I knew that I still had not fully processed Clint's passing and that I was grasping at anything and everything, even just a taste. I knew it, but familiar habits die hard if they die at all.

Which brings me back, once more, to Cal.

CHAPTER 28
I GOTTA MEET
THIS YAHOO

When I set out to write this book, I had no intention of writing as much as I have about Cal. While I knew that my relationship with him was both a confusing and defining one in my life, I had no idea just how big and how deep that impact was and continues to be. It is not the only thing I've learned in the process of releasing my skeletons from the closet and opening myself up.

Just to back up, I was so hurt after my relationship with him. For years. More years than I care to admit. I would have done anything for him. I tried so hard and gave so much of myself. Just like my father, despite all we went through, he just left me like it was nothing. And even as I reconnected and grew into other relationships, I was always left wondering why.

In my mind I was never a concern of his, and he always seemed so happy. I now understand, but for years this was such a big part of me. I wanted so badly for him to feel just once the pain that I was feeling all of the time. When I was younger, I often fantasized vividly about how I could possibly force this. I would play it over and over in my mind. He had a sliding glass door around the back of his house. His house was always dark and the drapes were always closed. The glass door opened to a plain, gray cement patio. I imagined myself knocking on the glass door and calling him outside. I would be standing there with a gun up to my head, and I would pull the trigger. The thought of this gave me such satisfaction. I believed that then and only then would he see how badly I was hurting. This, of course, is absolutely insane to me now! It is so difficult to even admit at this point in my life. Still, that's the level of pain I was feeling.

As I grew older, I turned all the pain I was feeling into determination. I was going to show him I could do the things he said I couldn't do. I remembered all the times he laughed at me and looked down on me. I was going to get out of that town and move to California and become a dancer. I was going to prove to him that I could make something of myself. He hadn't ruined me. I would show him.

I bring this up now because of the need to prove I never stopped. This included marrying someone such as Clint and raising a beautiful family. Trust me, I know how childish this sounds, but I always had an "I told you so, you didn't take me down" thought in the back of my mind. Getting Clint and this family proved that I had overcome him and the damage he had done...at least that's what I felt.

It took many years, but I eventually put the relationship into perspective, realizing what it was and wasn't, and dealing with the fallout, some of which I still have to work on today. Believe it or not, this happened with the help of Clint, who listened to me talk about Cal. He would sit back, listen, and observe. He would ask why I kept in touch with him, and why I had such motivation to prove him wrong. He managed to let me do what I needed to do to try to mend this life-long battle with myself, even when I didn't know exactly what I was doing or why.

So one night in 2006, while Cal was visiting Vegas with some childhood friends, I introduced him to Clint. I believe Clint's exact words were, "I gotta meet this yahoo."

Well, he did, and throughout the next few years they actually became friends. This felt a little strange, but I was still one up on Cal because friendship or not, I was the one who had Clint. At this point, Cal was a recovered addict. He had started his own business and needed advice. Since this was Clint's expertise, Cal respected him and reached out to him quite a bit. That's how they became friends.

Yes, life is bizarre. Never in a million years did I see all of us coming around like this. Regardless, through this, I actually made amends with Cal. I felt like all was fine.

Then Clint died.

I began regressing back to childhood behaviors and childhood thoughts. In came the tornado, and once again I was left broken and scattered. Only this time I wasn't sure if I could put the pieces back. It was not a good time for me to be thinking about Cal.

I soon became aware that he had written a book himself. Although I could not bring myself to read it in its entirety, I did know that "Kori Keefer" was mentioned on page twenty-four. In his story, he mentioned how my love and friendship helped him find some light in the darkness of his childhood. What a beautiful thing to say, right? Yes, it was. Had I not had years of built-up animosity to go along with the pain in my heart from losing the one man who *truly* loved me, it would have been an amazing thing to see. Instead, it confused the shit out of me.

What was he talking about? He never cared about me. I was just something in his way that he had to step over.

Soon, the bitterness and anger rose inside of me. I had never told him my side of what had happened between us. We had never discussed the feelings I had. I listened to him though, plenty of times. I put my balled up feelings aside, and I shoved them down just like everything else. I would think to myself, *Just be quiet and don't ruffle any feathers.* My whole life I had been quiet about everything.

I was so fucking tired of being quiet.

All this emotion started welling up inside and started rising to the surface. Although I do not remember exactly what was said, I do remember the argument. For the first time I spoke my mind to him. I was very angry because I didn't think Cal had given Clint the respect he deserved after his death. I believed he owed him this respect, he owed me this respect. The details of what was said don't even matter. It wasn't about any one thing. It was about a lifetime. And it all came out.

We didn't speak again for almost a year. When we finally did, like always, it was because I reached out to him. Once again I wanted to mend the relationship. I cannot explain why; I don't understand it myself. Still, for whatever reason, it was important to me that we patch things up, and we did.

So yes, he won again, but I didn't have enough fight left in me to care.

One morning I received a call from him. He told me he couldn't get Clint out of his mind. He told me he wanted to send the girls and me to Maui.

"I want to do this for you from Clint."

At first I told him absolutely not. I just couldn't imagine him spending that kind of money on us. Then he asked if I had ever been. I laughed and said yes, we were married there. Once he heard that, he became even more determined, and again, I didn't have the strength to put up a fight.

This would prove to be a significant trip.

Cal put us up at the Grand Wailea resort, on the opposite side of the island of where we were married. It had been years, and the resort we were married at had been knocked down. Something new was in its place. I was not particularly interested in going back to that side of the island anyway, so it was ok.

When we arrived, I was so happy to see the excitement on the girls' faces. It was just the five of us away together, and it felt so good to get a break from the pain. The plan was no plan. We would just go and explore. We had brought Clint's ashes in a backpack with us. I was waiting to find a special place to leave them. It had to feel right.

Hailey had one request while on the island, which was to jump off rocks somewhere, so I knew we had to make this happen. I spoke to a woman, and she told me of an amazing local spot where we could do this, but mentioned it was difficult to find. Sure enough, it was quite a drive even with the specific directions. The next morning as we were leaving the room, I almost forgot something. I called back for Hailey to grab Daddy. She put on the backpack with the ashes and off we went.

I would like to say that as we drove, things looked familiar, but they didn't. I had only been there once, and it had been about fifteen years. We followed the directions to the letter. We parked at what seemed to be quite a fancy hotel. We were to look for a stone walking path by the hotel and then a smaller dirt path that would wind around and eventually lead us to the local spot.

As we walked through the fancy hotel, we looked a little out of place. I told the girls to just act like they knew what they were doing and no one would say anything.

I'm beginning to realize that I used "fake it 'til you make it" as a strategy for many more things in my life than just a dance career.

They all played along just fine. We continued on and made our way out the back of the resort where there was a large patio and pool. And a beautiful view of the ocean. As we walked down some stairs, I began to feel something. I stopped and turned around to face the girls.

"Girls, do you know what?"

"What?" they all replied.

But I wasn't sure. Not totally. I turned back around and started walking again, saying, "I don't know."

"You are so weird!" They all laughed.

Just then, I stopped again. I looked straight out into the ocean. As I scanned the view, sure enough there it was. The two palm trees we stood between were still there. I didn't turn around to face the girls this time. I just stopped in disbelief.

"Oh my god, that's where we were married!" I yelled. I pointed it out to the girls, and they took off running.

I slowly walked to where they were. Along the way, I reminisced about the last time I had taken this very same walk. Only this time, it would be my four beautiful daughters waiting between the palms for me.

There was no doubt where we were going to leave his ashes.

We climbed down onto the rocks at the very end and inconspicuously poured him into the water. We then walked on to find the dirt path that led us to the most beautiful rock ledges. We spent the rest of the evening jumping and swimming while we quietly soaked in the most magical day we had experienced since Clint was gone.

Cal gave us that, and I am thankful. Without him, that experience would never have happened.

I don't think I'll ever fully understand this relationship. I think we're just two lost and longing souls that formed a bond a lifetime ago and sometimes coming together creates chaos. I'm still working on accepting it for what it is and what it isn't. I still have love for him. I still have grace and understanding. I still want to be friends with him. I still feel sorry for him in a number of ways. I also still want to prove myself to him. There are times I still have anger and frustration, not just because of our past, but what he sometimes continues to do, perhaps even unknowingly. He will still say beautiful things to me, but I've been manipulated before, and I question the sincerity behind what he says.

I know that he was and always has been a mysterious and sometimes dangerous connection in my life, but one that is there nonetheless. I don't know what the future holds for us as friends. I'm sure I'll find out quickly if he reads this. As long as we don't revert back to those old damaging behaviors, I think we'll stay in each other's lives and probably continue this confusing relationship. I hope we grow out of it, I really do. Until then, I will continue to process all I experienced with him over the course of my life, be grateful for the good times and the positive aspects of his friendship, and allow myself to be angry about the hurt and the pain.

I will also do my best to make sure my girls don't ever end up in the same situation as I did. Nor handle things the way I did. No, they deserve better and they will have better. They will have someone like Clint or no one at all.

My girls.

My beautiful girls.

CHAPTER 29
ONE BEAUTIFUL UNIT

My daughters lost their mother the same day they lost their father...and she was gone for a very long time.

It would take more than three years before I was able to get back to myself, to find clarity and the happiness and joy I felt about being a mother. If I'm being completely honest, I'm still in the process of finding her. I'm still working on recovering completely, to give them the mother they knew before Clint died.

They've missed her. I know they have. And they've suffered along the way.

I'll never get that time back, and in some ways, no matter what I do going forward, I know I'll never completely shake the guilt I feel in leaving them behind while I wandered aimlessly into the darkness of those first post-Clint years.

All I can do now is spend the rest of my life trying to make it up to them and being the best mother I can. It's a task I'm more than willing to take on.

The first part of that is acknowledging the mistakes I made.

To be blunt...I became a shell of their mother. I was here, I was loving them, but I didn't know how to help them through this, especially as I dealt with my own feelings and reversion back to the same bad habits. I was there, going through the motions and doing all I was capable of, but it wasn't enough. I was so swallowed up in my own pain that I didn't focus enough on helping to heal theirs. Like the true unique snowflakes that they are, they each handled their daddy's passing differently.

Hailey, the oldest, had a close bond with Clint, so she was definitely angry. Although I realized as an adult I should not take any of this personally, it was difficult. I could not get close to her. The way she looked at me made that quite apparent, and it kept me away from her. I didn't fight through it no matter how badly I just wanted to hold her like when she was a baby. I felt as if it was my fault. I came to believe that if there was a way to do a switch, she would have. It came up once when I tried to get close to her. I don't know why I even said it. In my childish behavior, I was hoping for a different response, but she couldn't give me what I wanted to hear. I told her that was ok, and I completely understood why she would feel that way. I told her how angry I was that this happened to her and I was so sorry for her pain.

I walked on egg shells around her for about a year. I really didn't know what to do. But the more I did this, the more distant our relationship became and the more it seemed ok for her to act this way. I understand better now. The more she pushed me away, the more I should have powered through. She needed that strength and protection that she had felt from him. I know that's what I wanted as a young girl, and it is scary to not have it.

It can also lead down a dangerous path. Around thirteen is when I began to fear that she was possibly going in the direction I had at that age. I worried more about her sneaking out, drinking, experimenting. Sure, it's normal behavior for a teenager, but she was clearly depressed and that's when those things become toxic... and a lifestyle.

That definitely brought the rage out in me. I had worked so

hard to create something amazing for my children, to not repeat any patterns.

I felt I was being punished for acting how I had. Yes, it was another example of me reverting back. I had Kevin drilling me to not parent from fear or based on my past experiences, but it was all that I could see.

Leila was so tight-lipped. There was no way was she going to show any emotion. She could not, and would not be broken open. I remember conversations with her, I saw emotion coming to the surface. I could just begin to see the pain. Her cheeks would turn red, her eyes would well up...and then just like that she would turn it off, swallow it down, and cover it up with her big beautiful smile. This scared me just as much as Hailey. I knew this was bad. I struggled constantly with how I was going to move this through her.

When it did, I wasn't ready.

At her year-end graduation from fifth grade, the kids all marched up to their spots in the rose garden at her school singing a lovely tearjerker song. She was standing in the front row. As they all got to their assigned spots, they turned to face us and finished the song. Everything she had been holding back that entire year came rushing up. Before she knew it or could stop it, out it came. There was nothing she could do to fight it back. I remember sitting in the audience not knowing what to do. She couldn't stop. What did I do? I just sat there frozen, my heart aching for her. Yet, I did nothing. Finally, her teacher walked over and consoled her. It took a little time, but she calmed down. To this day I could kick myself. Why didn't I go to her? She clearly needed me, and I sat there like an idiot. I have never even told her how sorry I was for that.

Not long after, I knew I had to find something that would give her a way to express herself. She had been taking dance for a few years, and I noticed at her last performance before Clint died that something had clicked. I knew what that meant to me when it happened. I remember sitting in the audience and thinking to myself, "Oh shit...she's got *it*." I eventually befriended a yoga instructor who taught at my studio. She was also an aerialist. I saw a performance of hers, and it was beautiful. I spoke to her about Leila and set up a private session with her. That's all it took; she was hooked. I believe that became her escape, her way to express herself, and to move through her pain. One Christmas, she performed live on stage at the Nobel Peace Prize ceremony in Oslo, Norway. As I watched on my computer (I couldn't leave as I was managing the yoga studio at the time) I was in tears, not just from the strength and beauty of her performance, but because she had found what she needed.

Sophia was just eight years old when Clint passed, yet she was the one I became emotionally dependent on. Somehow from the very beginning she could sense, even when we weren't around each other, that I was upset. Sure enough, she would seek me out and would appear at all the right moments. The night that he died, I believe she was the only one that fully comprehended what had happened. She understood, and she stayed awake with me for quite a while.

As time went on, it was as though she watched me out of the corner of her eyes, always making sure I was ok. That was a lot of stress to have on a little one's heart. The night I decided to go through his luggage, it was after I put the girls to bed. I wanted time to do it alone, and I didn't want the girls to know. I checked on all of them, and they were all sleeping. I went back to my room and shut the door. Maybe five minutes went by when there was a knock. I already knew who it was. I opened the door, and she observed what was happening. She didn't say a word as she walked over and knelt down beside me and gently started rubbing my back. We then went through all his things together.

This was one moment of many, and as time went on I soon hoped that she would find me when a moment of sadness hit. She would take one look at me and just know. She would stop whatever she was doing and come and lay with me. She wouldn't have to say a word. It is amazing what that did for me, and I actually feel selfish that I wanted this from her. It was almost as if she had to play parent for me, even as she was carrying around her own pain at such a tender age.

I'll never forget what she told me one time. "You know, Mommy, of course I wish I had Daddy back, but since I can't, I have to take notice of all the nice things people have done for us and all things we have been able to do that we wouldn't have done."

That took me a minute to process. This was probably one of the wisest things that I heard as we dealt with the effects of Clint's passing. I could barely imagine understanding that as a grown woman, let alone a child. A child, wise and emotionally connected beyond her years.

Sloan was just six when Clint died, and being so young, it was hard to gauge what she was feeling. She also doesn't have as many memories with him, and I know that hurts her just as much as it hurts me. Only now am I beginning to understand what's coming up in her. Sadly, she has spent many of her young years in fear of losing me. I created that fear, and even now, as things are better, she can't break that fear. I am still not sure how to get it through to her to not carry this weight around.

Sloan just always wanted to keep the peace. She still does. There have been many times where I have lost my temper, as much as I hate to admit it, and this has frightened her. She immediately tries to calm me down. She does anything she can to soothe me. I know she is so afraid of me having a heart attack. She knows that's how she lost Daddy so that has to be terrifying for a child. She will call me over and have me hug her, she will gently rub my back or my face, and tell me it's ok and to take a deep breath. This kills me.

But if I've taught them anything in the last few years, it's how losing your temper accomplishes nothing and how you'll end up having to pay for it later. I certainly am. I feel this could be a good tool for them to have.

From the moment I started having children, I feared them

turning out like me and making the same mistakes I did. When I was in my dark period after Clint passed, the fear overwhelmed me, and yet I was so consumed by my own pain and the repercussions of the bad choices I was making and the constant desire to just be numb to it all, I couldn't do anything about it.

What made it worse is that before this happened...I had been a great mother. I prided myself on it. It became my only mission in life. I was going to be the best mother I could, no matter the circumstances. They were always going to come first, and I would do whatever needed to be done.

But the reality is, as soon as tragedy hit, that person disappeared.

I have been clawing and scraping ever since to get back to that. While I am making significant progress, I still have a long way to go. All I can do is to continue to work at it, talk with them, be honest and hope and pray there aren't any long-term effects from my "time away."

Time will tell.

I am lucky to have them. They are all so unique, yet they work together as one beautiful unit. They are and always have been supportive as hell, often caring for me more than I care for them. It's just in their nature. They are four sweet souls, four strong little warriors. I know how lucky I am. I could have lost them.

Thank God they stayed with me, even as I went through my own shit and dealt not just with Clint leaving me and my own poor reactions, but also what he left behind.

CHAPTER 30
THE RAT

I think I've made it abundantly clear throughout the various chapters of this book, and my life in general, that I absolutely loathed and despised the restaurant business. Not only did it not work for me when I had to get a job in that industry, but it always seemed like a ton of work with very little reward. I never understood why it was Clint's dream to open Four Daughters Kitchen, why he was willing to sink so much time and money into it, why he was willing to deal with the nonstop headaches that came from it.

I would soon see that my hatred for the business could sink to even greater depths because the moment Clint died, I became the owner and operator of 4DK.

Yay.

Now don't get me wrong, I loved the restaurant because it was Clint's dream. But that's the thing. It was *Clint's* dream. Anyone who has ever run a restaurant can tell you that you need to have a true passion for it. If you don't, keep searching, because you really have to be ready to give up your life.

I did not have that passion. Not one bit.

When I became the owner, I soon realized that absolutely nothing could have prepared me. I could write a whole other book on what went on during those three years, but what would be the point? When you have someone with no business experience, no passion, no clue about the industry or running a business in general suddenly thrust into a leadership position, nothing good is going to come out of it.

Needless to say, I was lost. Not only that, I was burdened with this entity that I didn't want and all it did was add to the heavy loads I was already carrying on my shoulders. It frustrated me, depressed me, angered me...and I endured it for three years.

Three years I can't get back.

Three years where I should have been focusing on healing and getting my life back together.

Instead, I clung to it. I clung to it because it was Clint's dream and the girls' legacy. It was where they grew up, and it was a big part of their daddy.

How could I let that go? How could I take that away from them?

Turns out that by keeping it, I was also taking their mommy away from them.

When it came to this restaurant, I ignored every gut feeling I had from day one. I wanted out from the moment I jumped in...and that feeling never went away. I never once felt like I was getting the hang of it or finding my comfort zone. I was trying to quickly learn a skill overnight that people take years to develop while also trying to be a mother to four grieving girls. I thought I was busy before.

Plus, and maybe this is just how it goes, but it seemed like everything that could go wrong with that restaurant *did* go wrong. God love my husband, but he cut a lot of corners during the process of getting 4DK open. I'm sure it had to do with the budget, and that he did what he had to do to make it work. And it *did* work because he knew what he was doing.

But the operations were just messy and there was no clear

system in place for running it. You have two separate operations going on in a restaurant, front of the house and back of the house. It is very tricky keeping them both running smoothly, and it takes a certain person to know how to deal. Clint did as he spent most of his life working with people. He had a way about him. It didn't matter whether someone was being hired or fired, it always ended the same way, with a handshake and a hug.

I didn't really have that skill so the loosely held together operations started to crumble as soon as I took over. As I had to look into things more, I began to notice how much of the restaurant was being held together by duct tape. Also, guess who doesn't care that your husband died suddenly and you have four young children to keep on the straight and narrow?

The city, the state, the Board of Equalization, and the IRS. Business is business, and there is always someone watching.

The good news was the fact that the people who had been helping Clint run it were not going anywhere, at least for the first year and a half. Still, it wasn't enough. There was the constant weight on my shoulders that something would break down at the restaurant; or an employee might not show up, or someone might get in an argument and decide to leave during rush hour; or something could go wrong with the ordering of the food, or the freshness of the food, the cooking of the food; finding out a customer was not happy with something and reading about it on Yelp; the city fining me because I put up an umbrella to shade a customer from the sun but the umbrella wasn't in the original blueprints, or the fact that a chair might go past the invisible line on the sidewalk causing a pedestrian to have step around the chair, or too much noise in the evening, cameras not working, various systems freezing up, leaks in the ceiling, break-ins, theft, audits; and the bullshit melodrama of the employees, which started almost immediately upon me taking over; and on and on and on.

It just never ended.

I was over it before it even began, and yet I stayed for three of the longest and worst years of my life...even when I was getting constant signs to leave.

I have a dear friend and yoga mentor who I became quite close with in the years after Clint. Her name is Julie, and she has the gift of intuition. Believe it or not, Clint was the one who made this friendship blossom. I cannot fully understand this nor can I explain it, but I will never forget.

I was standing at the back of the restaurant, just a few days after returning from that fateful South Carolina trip and trying to get my bearings there. I noticed her walking toward me, and the expression on her face was serious. Looking back now, she must have been very uneasy knowing what she was about to say to me, someone she didn't know very well. At this point she could have no idea what my reaction would be. She began to tell me that the morning after he passed, he came to her. It was during the guided meditation portion of her class. She even described the very shirt he was wearing that night. He wanted her to tell me that he was good, and that he felt that he could help me more from where he was now. You can imagine how confused I was by this.

Are you fucking kidding me, how is that possible? How can he help me if he is not here? I need him HERE!

In the years to come, I learned that she had no choice. He would not leave her alone. She would call, text, or stop by the restaurant periodically to convey a message. As strange as this seemed in the beginning, I became quite comfortable imagining him with me all the time, using her as his voice. We would be having a normal conversation, then out of the blue she would tell me something he would say. On this one occasion, we were sitting at the bar in Four Daughters, and she began to laugh. I asked her what was so funny.

"He wants to know how bad this place has to get before you decide to sell it."

Around the same time, I started hearing noises from behind the walls in my house. I heard them all the time, for a couple months actually. Then I saw the bags of food in the pantry with holes in them and the containers chewed up.

I just let it be.

That should show just exactly how I exhausted I was with everything. I just did not have the time or energy to put any thought into what was going on behind the walls. I would soon find out that not one, not two, not three, not four, but five rats lived amongst us. One for each of us!

My mother was visiting, and she advised I do something about the obvious creatures living in the walls. I really remember thinking nah, they will just go away. It wasn't until she mentioned that one night Karma our dog came downstairs to the room she shared with Sophia and Sloan. She said she felt Karma at her feet. That would have been fine and dandy had that actually been the case...but Karma slept with me and never left my side. Soon after, I began to notice things like crumbs, droppings, wrappers on the counters and the couch, and of course, the pantry. I then began to develop a nervous tick because every time I walked into the kitchen in the evenings when the girls were in bed I would see one...whether on the counter, teetering on the edge of the cabinet door, or running across the floor over my foot and slipping into a hole under the cabinets. I then decided it was time to do something. It took me that long.

Funny enough, I found out that apparently there is meaning when a rat crosses your path.

According to a website on spirit animals, "Just because the Rat is small, do not think it's tiny in power. In fact, a Rat Spirit Animal may be telling you to take back your mojo and defend your territory. Either that or Rat warns that your situation is sinking fast and it's time to get out! To discern which, watch the behavior of your animal spirit guide. The more urgent they appear, the more likely it is that the time to move is NOW."

Ironically enough, Cal was the one who had sent me the info on the symbology of the rat, but this ended up having significant meaning to me. The restaurant that I was clinging to for no other reason than the connection with Clint had become such a source of bad energy for me. It was going down quick and taking me with it. Who was I kidding? This was his dream, not mine and I was killing myself. The final decision was made. The restaurant had to go.

Maybe those rats were sent to open my eyes!

Getting out––like everything else with the restaurant––was no walk in the park. Even after I sold it, the state wouldn't release the funds until I gave them $50,000 for an audit back in 2013. There were many meetings with them with tears in my eyes, literally unable to answer their questions because I simply didn't know. It was the final "fuck you" from that place.

I did, and in some ways still do, feel bad that I had to let Clint's dream go, but it just wasn't for me. On a side note, the restaurant's name will live on forever as it gets mentioned in the song "DNA" by Kendrick Lamar, who was a frequent patron. It was pretty cool seeing him sing a lyric about Four Daughters Kitchen live on stage at the 2018 Grammys! When I think of that moment, I can't help but think of Clint and how excited he would have been to hear the name drop.

When all was said and done, and I had a moment to step back and reflect, I realized that the restaurant, beyond adding to the tremendous stress I already had in my life, was making me somebody I wasn't and that I didn't want to be. The way I know this is because from the moment I sold it and all the bullshit was over, I began to feel alive again. Yes, I was still very angry that I had wasted three years of our lives, but I actually began to feel more... clear.

For the first time since that dark night that I lost my husband, I wondered if I could dare to hope.

CHAPTER 31
AND THAT'S
PROGRESS

Selling the restaurant was one of a number of things that seemed to happen all at the same time. Once that weight was lifted, it brought clarity to some other issues in my life. Everyone who has experienced a fall or a tragedy or a loss of self (haven't we all in some way?) can tell you that there is a moment when things come together, when there is a convergence of all the different facets of your life that are in turmoil and you can step outside of yourself and see them for what they are. That is when you make the choice. Do I continue the descent or do I say enough is enough and pick myself up off the mat?

I needed the burden of the restaurant out of my life. I wasn't being the mother I needed to be for my girls. I needed to look for something more in the men I was spending time with while at the same time not worrying so much about keeping Clint or his memory on such a pedestal. I was drinking way too much and then knocking myself out every night with Ambien, which was no way to live my life. I had fallen hard back into my eating disorder...and I needed to start being honest about it, not just with myself but with those who loved me.

I was no longer the woman I had worked so hard to become.

I needed help.

Luckily, during all of this, I had kept in touch with and continued to see Kevin, my therapist, regularly. What this man had to endure in those sessions, especially as things started opening up, I wouldn't wish on anyone. But he stuck with me and helped me and eventually, after quite a few sessions, a lot of tears, some yelling and screaming, and all around rage and a ton of personal work...we started to see some progress.

First you become aware of the issues.

Then you work to relieve yourself of them.

I opened up about everything I was experiencing, from continuing to miss Clint and the anger that sometimes surrounded that, to the restaurant, the girls, the men, the drinking, and even the eating disorder.

And that's progress.

As the sessions with Kevin went on, I decided to see where else I could get some added help. Kevin also recommended I see someone else a bit more experienced in dealing with eating disorders and the emotional strain tied around that. That's when I decided to try an EMDR session.

EMDR stands for Eye Movement Desensitization and Reprocessing. It's a pretty hard core therapy treatment to help relieve psychological stress. There are many schools of thought on the validity of EMDR, and I don't want to make a case for any of them. All I can do is share my experience of what happened in my sessions.

EMDR is a type of therapy that can possibly take you deeper than talk therapy. But in order for it to work you have to be willing to feel your feelings, which was always tough for me. It is good for releasing trauma. It's kind of like opening the gate for a feeling or a thought. It allows for a feeling that was tucked down deep to rise to the surface and become something we can set free. Once this happens, we are able to release whatever it is.

It didn't work for me right away. Every time I showed up for a session, I wasn't open enough to actually go through with the actual EMDR treatment. It took about eight sessions of us just talking before I was ready.

That's when something amazing happened.

When I entered the room for that session, my therapist Linda could feel my energy right off the bat. She even commented on the fact that I was usually a ball of energy with one foot out the door the whole time. I didn't laugh at this. Normally I would in order to make the person feel at ease. I just sat there, slumped in the corner of the couch, staring at her. She asked what was going on with me that day. I told her I was at a loss, and that I didn't know what I was doing. For the most part, I have really worked on not going to that place of fear, not getting anxiety about raising the girls without Clint, about how to reinvent myself and make a living.

But for some reason it got the best of me on this day. Toward the end of the session she asked if I would like to try the EMDR. As of yet, I hadn't experienced the feelings that would allow us to move forward with this type of therapy. On that day, for whatever reason, I definitely was allowing myself to feel. So of course, I insisted.

She asked me where I was emotionally on a scale of one to ten, ten being the highest or most intense emotional feeling and one being the lowest.

"Well I know things can always be worse, so I will go with a nine," I replied. She then asked me to cover my right eye with my right hand. She then asked four personal questions. Without hesitation, the answers came. I didn't even have to think. I immediately began to cry.

"What do you picture?"

"I see Clint from the neck down. I don't see his face, but I know it is him."

"What are your feelings?"

"I feel a numbing pain, like a loss of strength, almost a limp sensation in my entire body."

"What are your thoughts around what you see?"

"I used to be safe. I am not safe anymore."

"What are your emotions?"

"I am so sad. I am alone. I am scared."

She let me sit with this for a few moments as I cried painful tears. Then she asked me to cover my left eye with my left hand. She continued with the same four questions. It was as if a switch had been flipped. Maybe a second had passed, but that was it! I immediately began laughing, like deep from the belly laugh. I told her the only thing I pictured was the actual painting that was hanging on the wall behind her. I felt absolutely nothing! All the pain, all of the feelings of loneliness and sadness were completely gone for the moment! She let me sit with this for a few moments, as I sat enjoying what I was feeling. Then she stuck her hands up in the air, shrugged her shoulders, and said, "I don't know what to say, it works!"

I sat there in disbelief. Finally, I said, "What the fuck just happened?"

It was over an hour drive back to Manhattan Beach. I basically drove the car on autopilot while I deeply contemplated what I had experienced. I tried to replay it to understand. This was when I realized that I never truly allowed myself to feel the loss of Clint. I had bouts of sadness, but it became such a habit to cut the feelings off as soon as they came. Eventually, my mind just did it on its own. Add in my whole approach of "don't eat, don't feel" and that was how I survived. That wasn't healthy.

I read a story once about a woman who did some deep soul searching of her own. As I read what she went through, I could not quite grasp what she was talking about. She spoke of how hard it was to dig deep within and how angry she became upon discovering her own realizations. I did not understand what she was speaking of. How do you not know who you are? Do you not realize your own personality, your own choices as you are living your life? Well, I soon realized that most of us don't. I know I didn't. When I began this process and really started to see myself, I became very angry. In the weeks to come I began observing me. It was like taking a back seat to myself as I moved through my life. I observed my thoughts, my actions, my reactions, my innate behaviors. I forced myself off of autopilot, which is how I have lived most of my life, especially over the years since Clint passed.

I was not always living from truth or authenticity. During this time, I had molded myself into what someone else wanted. When I say "someone," I am mainly speaking of men. Imagine a chameleon always changing colors depending on its environment. That was me. I did whatever I needed to do to get acceptance and to hopefully get love. I thought back to all the times I compromised myself, when I made things ok that clearly weren't, just because I wanted love.

Upon this realization, I went dark in my mind for a quite a while. I had a difficult time even cracking a smile. And it was noticed. I didn't care, I just couldn't do it anymore. Everything I was, all that I was doing for the sake of this façade, to chase a false kind of love, took so much energy, and I was done with it.

You fucking dumbass, why don't you love yourself more? Why do you allow this? Why are you so weak? You are raising four daughters who don't have a father to guide them, to love them, and to protect them. It's up to you! Be a strong woman!

I had gone back to behaving, thinking, and feeling like I did before Clint. I had a break where I (mostly) got to be myself because he loved me the way I was, freak show and all. Even still, I was not able to tell him all my "things," because I was ashamed and afraid he would see me in a different light. I was so blind! I now look through all the amazing cards he gave me. He didn't just walk into Hallmark and grab any card! It was obvious he took the time to pick the ones with the words that showed how he felt.

He wrote me beautiful poems, expressing how much I meant to him, how much having me as a wife and mother to his children had made him stronger, how much he couldn't imagine his life without me. I cannot say enough how saddened I am that I didn't realize this at the time. I don't remember reading these beautiful words that he wrote, and if I did remember, they clearly didn't sink in. That's a regret I'll always carry with me.

In the month that followed that session, I began to just sit and really process these things, everything about me, Clint, my feelings on love, my needs, habits, my being a mother...everything. It all began to unfold right before my eyes. For the first time I understood why I did the things I did. I began to understand why I allowed the things I allowed. Why I felt the things I felt. I also saw that Kevin had been trying to explain this to me for quite a while, but we all hear what we are able to hear in the time we are able to hear it. Sometimes it takes longer to grasp.

This was a long, slow difficult process of bringing things up and letting go, and each time I did this, I began to see the light. It was still far off, but it was there. It was as if a tiny flame was lit and I could feel it's warmth inside of me. From this feeling I was able to go deeper. Each time I felt the relief it gave me, the more I had the motivation and drive to go further. The further I went, the more I let go, the tiny flame became a fire. It is burning inside of me non-stop now, and I refuse to ever let it go out.

We feel if we allow ourselves to feel. We don't feel if we don't allow ourselves to feel. It is that simple. It is a choice we make. The question is, do we want to do the work it takes to drudge up these things that keep us chained?

The answer is, yes we do.

Or at least, yes I do!

And it all started with me letting go...

Of everything. Not just what happened post Clint's passing, but all of it, from the time I was a little girl on. I had to face it, accept it, own up to it, deal with it, and let it go. What came next was the one thing I've always been chasing.

Happiness.

I feel that when we train ourselves to shove things down, we stunt our growth on a conscious level. We continue to do this over and over, adding layer upon layer. Most of us live our entire lives here in this state of being, and it becomes difficult to claw back and eventually break through, but it is possible, no matter your life circumstances. The more I wanted this and was willing to stick with it, the greater the reward when I succeeded. It took me almost four years of constant work, and I'm still working. I can't stress that enough. I can honestly feel my heart...it's like an open wound exposed to air for the first time. I truly am feeling everything for the first time. I also see Clint in everyone, and I feel him in every moment. Although it often hurts, I am happy to be in this place. I have accepted. I have surrendered. I am here.

Which leads me once again to the Divine Order. I saw an article once about how the Universe has a system that works. It said the sun and the moon know exactly what to do. The ocean waves are constant, and the flow of nature is what is happening. Human evolution is a beautiful and profound system as well; yet, as humans our lives are full of chaos.

I lived in chaos most of my life because my mind only focused on what I thought I needed: made up lies to (falsely) better protect myself. Being present in life could be so simple if we would just take the time to see, to hear, to feel, to touch, to smell, to taste. Nature can only do so much to guide us. We need to listen. It begins with a feeling, a true authentic feeling that will guide us in the correct direction, if we choose to take it. I see that now.

I believe this Divine Order led up to our last night with Clint. In June, Clint quit his job, and spent the next two months enjoying us, the beach, and volleyball. In July, he decided last minute to fly to Tucson and spend the weekend with his family. In August, we all flew to South Carolina to see my side of the family who we hadn't seen in six years. We were there for one week, perhaps the best week we've all ever had. The night before we were supposed to return home, we took the most amazing photos and had an unbelievable dinner together, basking in the love of our entire family. That night, Clint asked me to sit on his lap; he asked me if I was comfortable; we connected in our love one last time; and he passed. Those things all happened in that order for a reason, and it's just taken me some time to see it.

I feel that Divine Order is playing out in my overall life as well. I can see it even more clearly as I've worked on this book. I see the patterns, the things that have happened that have led me to who I am, both when I've been false and when I've been my authentic self. I see the circumstances that have led me to the bad choices and the pain as well as my part in them. I see what needed to happen to get me to where I am now and how those things came together. I see that once again, it all comes down to me. I have the choice. I can move forward with happiness. After the EMDR session and several breakthroughs with Kevin, this became my new mission. It still is and it will be until the day I die. I believe in all of it, and I get excited about continuing the work.

And there is still a lot of work, as I proved during the process of writing this book, even after I had my realization and awakening. It's one thing to believe and to preach, it's another to practice. It never ends. I wake up most days sad that Clint is gone, but then I check in with myself, making sure I'm avoiding those familiar pitfalls and preparing myself to go forward through the day. Within that process, I found happiness.

But I do still stumble...so now would be a good time to tell you about my breasts.

CHAPTER 32
SO I GOT BOOBS

The next relationship I fell into was rather by accident. Once again, I really wasn't looking. But I guess I would say his persistence paid off. Also, it was so easy for me because I felt there was just a comfort with having someone else instead of being alone. So next thing I knew, there I was, involved again...and on my way to a very bad decision, but one of the more eye-opening experiences of my life.

Before I go on, I just have to say...poor Herb. That was his name, and although he didn't know it yet, he was going to end up having to take the wrath of all my choices up to then. He didn't know what hit him. Imagine a bunch of kids in a candy store and all of them but one steal some candy and run out the door. The one kid left gets the blame.

Herb was that one kid.

Even though I was waking up to my truth, and confronting essentially a lifetime's worth of revelations, I was still in a vulnerable place. I wasn't healed, I was "in process," and that left me wide open, allowing for chaos to occasionally take over. Simply put, when you're going through that kind of an awakening, you're not necessarily in the best place to make wise decisions.

I knew from the beginning that he was a wonderful man, another great father to his children. Despite our differences, which I actually used to tease him about, we began dating...and there I went again. I became a chameleon and changed things up to match what he wanted, or (even worse) what I *thought* he wanted. Despite the progress I was making, I still wasn't strong enough in my own skin to be my own person.

Shortly after we started dating, there were some little things I noticed that made me think he liked women who were a little more endowed than me. Some of my old childish paranoia took over and I started to test the waters. I would joke about my own smaller breasts by putting myself down, so to speak. When his responses were anything different than, "You look great the way you are" I began thinking that maybe I should get mine enhanced.

I know, I know, but again, learning and practicing are two different things. I had years of a habit to break, of adhering my life to this constant need of love and affection.

My mind was made up quickly. Some women spent years researching and thinking about this. Not me. We started dating in October, and my breasts were a size A. By Christmas, I was a D cup.

A quick aside here to make it crystal clear that I don't blame him one bit for any of this. First of all, he had absolutely no idea everything I was going through. We hadn't gotten that far in our relationship. When I told him everything much later, after the fact, he was in shock. While he may have been my unwilling cata-lyst, making the choice to do this was *all* on me and my inability to truly listen to my gut. Herb and I are still very good friends, and we will be for life. I now look at him as somebody who helped me make the absolute best mistake of my life and we can laugh about that!

But not at first. No, there was no laughing.

As I woke up from surgery, I looked down and found myself staring at these large breast implants that felt quite heavy sitting on my chest. This would have been cool, maybe, had I actually wanted them! I immediately had a churning in my stomach. It's when I woke up literally and figuratively.

What the fuck did I just do?

Over the next week I realized I now had to live with these. That is when I fell into an angry hole for quite a while. I knew I had made a huge mistake. They were a constant reminder of my weakness, even as I was doing all this positive work. Every time I stood up, or got a glimpse in the mirror, I was reminded. I tried so hard to talk myself into them, but there was no getting comfortable and I just grew more and more angry. I fought with wanting them out the moment I had them.

I even went back in and asked about removing them when I was four months post op. They told me it was way too soon. I was stuck with them. To make things worse, for someone who has struggled her whole life with body issues, when I got the implants, it made me feel like my entire body was bigger. It really messed with my head, especially as I was finally owning up to and trying to combat my eating disorder.

I was also really embarrassed by them. For one year, I just tried to hide myself as much as possible, which was rather difficult as a yoga instructor. I acted fine, as I always did, so no one would have realized how uncomfortable I was. Picking out shirts to wear was a nightmare. I couldn't wear anything I had.

One of the worst was showing up to see Kevin after I had them done. For a while, I avoided him entirely. Then I just showed up in his office one day hiding behind a big shirt. I plopped down on his couch and said in a very angry tone, "So I got boobs."

"Ok, you had a breast augmentation, would you like to talk about it?" he asked, concerned that this was yet again a return to old behaviors.

"Nope."

This was a pattern for whenever I was making a wrong choice. I would stay away from Kevin as he was my voice of reason. I would avoid going in, make something up and cancel an appointment. Eventually though, I would have to make my way back and go through an embarrassing explanation. I would always feel so foolish.

But the worst was revealing them to the girls...and yet, I'm grateful. These ridiculous breasts led to one of the more cathartic moments we all had since Clint died. It started with an explosion...

Honestly, this whole thing had to really confuse them. What was Mommy doing and why? I did not put much time into preparing them or me. That was always my way: Do it, then figure it out. In this case, it completely backfired, and I paid the price.

I know the littles (Sophia and Sloan) had to have been freaked out by my decision to do this, but they would never say anything except, "Mommy, you are beautiful" or "They look fine, Mommy."

The older gals were not that forgiving. Hailey just came straight out and said, "They are too big." Leila, in different words, agreed. This all came to a head one night. We were out to dinner, and I was having a bad night. I hated being in my body with these things. I was missing Clint, and I just wanted him to fix everything. As we were sitting there, Hailey blurted out, "So are you going to walk around with your cleavage showing like all the Manhattan Beach moms?"

That was all it took. We were sitting at the table, and the tears started welling up. Sloan was across the table. She took one look and saw something was not right. She immediately came over to me. "Mommy, it's ok. Mommy, what's wrong?" Sophia followed right after her. I couldn't stop myself. The flood gates opened, and I had to leave the table and go into the bathroom to try and gain some composure.

My mom was with us, and she was very upset. I know she said a couple words. The littles followed me in the bathroom, but it was no use. I couldn't stop. I couldn't fake being ok, and I hated the concern on the girls' faces. We left to go back home. I couldn't even look at Hailey. I immediately went in my room, and the littles followed, trying so hard to calm me down. Next Leila came in, and soon after Hailey. Then...I lost it and the words came flying out. "Do you have any idea how hard this is for me? I am trying so hard to do what is right! It breaks my heart that you lost your daddy, but I lost him too! I have no idea what you think about me, as a mother and the choices I have made. Maybe you think it's horrible that I dated someone else! No one will replace daddy. My heart is broken! I want him back so bad! But I am so lonely, and I am so scared, and I am doing the best I can with all of you!"

Suddenly everybody was crying. It was awful, painful, and yet... beautiful. Those were the times that the realness of our situation and all the vulnerability blossomed. The walls that separated us came down. Those were the ties that bound us. It was the vulnerability that we were able to show along with the truth we were able to confess that continued to make us stronger. We have grown together as a unit, and all five of us have each other's backs. This was one of several much-needed moments to remind each other that we were all hurting together and that we all loved each other. So, in that respect, maybe the boobs weren't such a bad thing.

No, they were.

I saw all the choices I have made. Because of wanting to please others or wanting acceptance or wanting to not upset someone. I also began to see how these decisions affected me for the worse.

That was the *true* wake-up call.

Originally I thought I had made the choice so I was stuck with them and better get used to them. For a whole year, all I could think was that I had to spend the rest of my time here feeling uncomfortable in my own skin.

Then I thought...why?

One day, I randomly showed up to a spin class early and started talking to the instructor about my implants and how much I hated them. The spin instructor opened up to me about her problems with her size and turned out she was just as uncomfortable as me. We went a couple months trying to boost each other up. Then one day she said she would be going in for her fourth surgery, and although she had other complications, she was also going to go smaller. It turned out to be a huge relief for her.

Part of the problem was still speaking up for myself. Going and talking to the doctor was a very uncomfortable thing for me because the request was quite silly. Although too big for me, they actually did look really good. Then one day, Kevin said, "Kori you have to start advocating for yourself." That really sunk in for some reason. So I went in and discussed options. It was back and forth nonstop on whether to replace them with smaller ones or just take them out completely. This time I listened to my gut. I just wanted them out.

I wasn't sure how they would look, but I decided I had to be ok with it because I knew I couldn't go on like this anymore, I just wanted to feel comfortable in my own skin again. The morning of, I think I arrived thirty minutes early. They couldn't get me on the table fast enough. I woke up in the recovery room and immediately I could feel a difference. Obviously, I was a little sore. That didn't bother me one bit...because the weight was no longer there. And I mean that in every possible way. I seriously cannot express how good it felt to have them out. It was almost like the whole experience taught me the biggest lesson of all, one that has taken me my whole life to grasp.

I need to be comfortable in my own skin.

I need to be like those strong girls I was always envious of.

I need to advocate for myself, speak up, and not care or worry so much about what others will think or say.

I need to accept me, be me, love me.

Just like Clint did.

I now focus on putting all I've learned, all that theory, into loving practice.

CHAPTER 33
WHERE EXACTLY
AM I NOW?

I feel like it would be very strange to end this book with a chapter on my breasts. Then again, those who know me probably wouldn't be a surprised by it. And maybe after reading about my life and how I traveled through it, you wouldn't be surprised either.

What's funny is that catharsis or an awakening always comes in the most unexpected places at the most unexpected times. After everything I've gone through, that which I did to myself and that which was done to me, and after every mistake I've made, every step forward I've taken, everything I've desired, hurt, helped, created, lost and loved, after everything I've learned, the big realization, the big eye-opening moment really came in the wake of my breast surgery.

The Divine Order can be funny that way.

As I wrap things up, I also realize that this book has been part of that process as well. There's a reason that I needed to write this and write it now. Sure, I wanted to maybe help others who have dealt with loss, tragedy, and with bad choices and circumstances. I also wanted to leave a legacy for my girls, to give them some clarity into who their mom is and maybe why as she's tried to be the best mother possible for the four most amazing girls in the world. But mainly, I needed to write this to put my life in perspective, to help answer the multitude of questions that I have, to help acknowledge and move on from the mistakes I've made, and to help me make sure I don't make them again.

As egotistical as this sounds, I also needed to do it to celebrate me, and I'm worthy of that.

I don't know exactly what I've learned in this process. There are a few things, but I think the rest will come over time. I do know that writing this has helped me connect with my past and my present. It's worked like a circle—I've felt something, put it down on paper, looked at it, and then took it back in, absorbing and processing it. That's healthy. I'm eager to see what else happens now that it's written, especially in terms of how I feel.

So....where exactly am I *now*?

Well, I have opened my mind over the last four years. This has been very difficult work on my part, but I've stayed persistent and I will continue to do so. After a while I started noticing a change in my thinking, in my emotions, and in the way I dealt with not only myself but different situations. Slowly I noticed I was taking on more of a "Clint" view. I am so much calmer now, I don't react quickly the way I used to. I am in a place of acceptance of whatever *is*. I live with a sense of peace in knowing everything is working in the direction it is supposed to. I would say Clint is with me, but I believe the word "in" or "a part of me" would better describe how I feel. There isn't a day that goes by that I don't have to talk myself out of the sadness of what we lost, but the good news is, I can.

I am thankful because I live so differently now. The biggest thing I am grateful for is the time I am spending with the girls. Not that I didn't appreciate it before, but I am just more present with them and more aware of what that means.

I now realize the importance of doing what is authentic to me, not because I should do something. On that note, I'm also working on giving myself some more credit. Yes, I've made mistakes, but who hasn't? I am tough; I am strong; I am confident. I *am* one of those girls I was always envious of. And really, I have always been this way, even if it was hiding under the surface. I just never put myself on that pedestal. Clint did though. He knew these things about me, and he has finally gotten through to me! It's only a shame that it took his death to make me see.

I of course still miss him each and every day. That will never go away. I am just as much in love with him today as I was when we started building our life together. I am grateful for not only the time we had, but also what he showed me and what he gave me in these beautiful girls. I see him in all four of them.

Also, Clint is still a very big part of our everyday lives. I'm not just talking about what he taught us, the love he showed, and the experiences we shared with him.

No, he's literally still here. He is definitely with us, guiding us.

I would like to tell you about Clint's very old, cheap, Casio digital watch. He wore this watch all the time, even with his nice work suits. Instead of wearing the face on the top of his wrist, like a normal person, he wore it so he had to turn his wrist up to see the time. Clint knew me to be very impatient. I didn't wear my own watch, so I was always asking him the time. There was a button you could press that would light up the screen to see the time.

At least, that's how it was supposed to work. Lying in bed, when it was dark, I would reach over to press the button so the time would light up. It never worked. It was also very possible I was pressing the wrong button. Nonetheless I would get very irritated. "How come this never works?" He would reply, in his very soothing calm voice, "You just do this." He would gently press the button and the light would turn on.

When he passed, this watch became permanently affixed to my

wrist, and I wore it just like he did. Cut to the two-year anniversary when me and the girls were visiting my sister in South Carolina and visiting the exact same house where he passed. My sister had reached out to the owners to see if we could stop by. I wanted to see what it would feel like to be back in that house. I wanted to feel that pain again, perhaps to let it go. I thought it would be powerful for me, but in our short visit to that house, it wasn't.

Anyway, on the anniversary day, Kelly and I decided to go take a yoga class. I know this seems weird but we drove to the same studio and took the same class and even put our mats in the same spots they had been two years prior. Honestly this wasn't planned, it just worked out that way. I was feeling very somber as I walked in the room. I was trying to remember how I felt that morning before my life changed, but that was impossible to recreate.

The yoga class was great, then again yoga always makes me feel great. We grabbed our things and went back to her house. I started packing because we were set to go home the next morning. Just like my last night with Clint, I began running around from room to room gathering all our things. At one point, as I walked into my bathroom which was very dark, I noticed something out of the corner of my eye. For a moment I thought I was crazy, but I swore I saw Clint's watch light up. I immediately stopped and looked again. Sure enough, it lit up.

I thought to myself that possibly it lights up in the dark and I just never noticed it before. Of course that was my mind trying to make sense of something because that is what it always does. I walked in and out of the bathroom a few more times to see if it would light up again. It did not. I figured it was just a fluke and went back to packing. There it went again, and again. Then it would stop and then go again. I ran downstairs to tell Kelly. I kept pointing it out to her, "Look, there it is again!" We both stood there in disbelief. This continued the rest of the day. I could not keep this to myself, I had to tell the girls!

Also, Kelly kept a very clean house. When we were there two

years before, she walked into the room where Clint was standing. He was leaning to one side with his hand pressed right smack-dab in the center of the glass window. She told me she laughed and thought to herself "Only Clint would place his hand right in the center of the glass like that." Shortly after he died, one rainy day as she was walking by, she saw his hand print. It was clear as day, and it looked like he was waving. She immediately sent me the picture of it. She decided not to wash that window, ever.

I called the girls downstairs. I pointed the watch out to them. We stood there and contemplated his presence. As I looked up, I noticed the outside light was shining perfectly through the glass. Clear as day, we could see Clint waving at us.

Later, as I climbed into bed, I noticed that the entire screen on the watch was blank. No time, no date, no day was shown. I immediately got a sinking feeling in my stomach, as I assumed the watch was probably just on its way out. That would explain it. I turned the light out and went to bed. I woke up in the middle of the night as I always did. I knew the watch was broken, but I thought for old time's sake I would press the button one last time. To my surprise it lit right up with the time, date, and day.

Three years later his watch now sits faceless on my night-stand next to my bed. But not always. Everyday at some point I will glance over at it, and occasionally more times than not, it will be working. The time. The date. The day. This is just one of many coincidences that remind us daily that he is still with us...

I am now finally at peace with everything that happened. There is no need to look back anymore. Believe it or not, I am so happy for all of my experiences because they have led me here, and despite everything, I would do it all again. Buddha said, "Every experience, no matter how bad it seems, holds within it a blessing of some kind. The goal is to find it." It took me some time, but I finally did.

Speaking of peace, the stability I had been looking for my entire life was within me all along. I was the key. I still am. I am the love that I've been looking for my whole life and it feels amazing being wakened to that fact after having been unconscious my entire life. The truth will set you free. I cannot express enough the sense of lightness I have felt by letting go, and how this has propelled me forward. It has given me new life.

I believe that we are here for one reason and one reason only. Happiness. The challenge is to find happiness no matter what curveball this life throws. We are meant to be happy. We are capable beyond belief, but we get lost along the way. I said earlier that I began writing as a form of healing. During this process, I began to accept myself as I am, rather than who I thought I should be.

Every day I start again. Every moment, I now check in. For me that is the only way to live with joy. There is more to life than to live with sadness, pain, anger. Yes, these things are always just below the surface, and I let these feelings be a constant reminder, almost a gift actually, of how I want to live the rest of my time here, however long or short that may be. I know I feel much better when I am present and by being present I now see and feel all the blessings that my life holds. That brings the happiness.

This sounds so cliché, but I am excited about every day because it is new and it gives me a chance to start again. There is so much for me to look forward to and to be happy for, but the only way for me to do this is to stay present in the knowing of it. I am excited because it is kind of fun to not know what the future holds but at the same time to work toward the endless possibilities.

So here I am. I am happy in knowing that I can choose my happiness at any time. I am happy in knowing that I can guide my girls to this truth and they can find their way having these tools to help them. And I'm not talking about little flashes of joy. I mean overall happiness. To live fully is to choose happiness, no matter our circumstances.

This day and every day, I choose to be happy.

With that in my heart, mind, and soul, as I paddle out into the wide and wild ocean before me, I do so with a loving smile. Clint's smile, my girls' smile, my smile. My happiness.

To My Beautiful Girls
Hailey, Leila, Sophia, and Sloan.

I cannot begin to tell you how in awe I am of each of you. You were given the biggest challenge that I could have ever imagined. So sudden, so life changing.
Each of you, in your own way, not only accepted this but so graciously persevered.
I can only imagine what your little hearts were feeling and the thoughts your young minds were thinking. I contemplate this a lot because I now realize that a big part of me died that day as well.
I truly feel that the mother you had grown so accustomed to was gone for quite a while. Although this pains me whenever I think about it, I try not to hold on to any regrets from this. I know I survived the only way I knew how at that time.
I also realize that a big part of my survival was because of you. I have learned from all of you what it means to be strong. I need you to know this because there were times when I really didn't see a point of any of this without him.
But there you all were, and a part of him is in all of you.
I know it goes unsaid that there will always be a huge piece missing, and I know you feel this. There isn't a moment that goes by that he is not a part of.
I am beyond grateful for you, my beautiful girls. I truly love you more than life. Most of all, it gives me such great happiness to know you will always have each other. I know that dreams come true because my whole life I dreamed of him and I have dreamed of you.

Like the inscription in Daddy's wedding ring, I love you...Always and Forever, Mommy

Dear Clint
Daddy.

Even after all this time, I still have these moments that I cannot believe you're really gone.

What I would give to be wrapped in your arms just one more time. I often think back to that day and I am so sorry that I didn't do more for you. I knew something was off. Even in our last moment together, before that one big breath, you asked if "I" was comfortable. Let me tell you now, I was more comfortable than you will ever know.

You were a dream come true. With all my insecurities hidden deep, and the choices that could have taken me down many different paths, I was still led to you.

I never told you this, but there were times you would show up unexpected wherever I was. I would notice you, and my heart would literally drop into my stomach. Yes, even after eighteen years your big, goofy, handsome self still did that to me. To be honest, I know I did that to you as well.

The girls and I miss you so much. We talk and laugh about you all the time. I truly believe you would be proud of your basketball team. We are a force to be reckoned with! It's amazing how strong we have become. We were faced with the unimaginable, and although we have had many challenges along the way, we have powered through. The resilience never ceases to amaze me. We did this, you and I; we built this team together.

I have grown so much because I had to. These past few years have been the most difficult years of my life, and I owe you so much for helping me to find these qualities that I now realize I possess. I love who I have become. I am different in so many ways. I can laugh about this because although I don't recognize me, I know you would. You knew what I was capable of, you always did.

My promise to you is to live everyday with

the strength in knowing you are here with me, always on my right side, like Julie said.

I loved you from the moment I met you, and even though I had to say it first, I know you did too. And yes I am still giving you shit for that!

Thank you for the funny memories. They truly carry us through. And now more than ever, thank you for our beautiful four daughters.

Always and Forever,
Kori...Mommy

Dear Kori,

I want to tell you how sorry I am for the way I have treated you all these years.

Your entire life you have put up with me not only hurting you physically but even more so mentally.

I can picture you as a child, those big beautiful innocent brown eyes so full of love. Love and acceptance was all you wanted from me, and I am deeply sorry for not giving this and for not helping you believe that you were worthy of these things. My constant chatter always telling you in endless exhaustion how you weren't good enough or deserving enough. And those moments of happiness that I just stole away from you as quickly as I could because I didn't want you to be happy for too long. I thought you needed to know that the other shoe would always drop, and I wanted to prepare you for that.

All these things I did and said to you were so unnecessary and hurtful, and I am truly sorry for this burden I have put on you.

I want you to know that I now realize how wrong I was in making you think this way and now that I am aware I will be here to constantly remind you how much I love you.

I just ask one thing of you...let's not look back anymore. So much lies ahead for you, and I will be here by your side every step of the way. Trust in me now, and with this second chance you have so graciously given me, I will not let you down.

Always and Forever...from now on,
Kori

ACKNOWLEDGEMENTS

Thank you to...

Hailey, Leila, Sophia, and Sloan...for choosing me. I don't know where I would be without you.

Mom...for always being the support I need and for the unconditional love that I have learned to know.

Kelly...for your endless loving guidance that has not fallen on deaf ears. I hope you will run with this gift.

Jason...for being my loving brother and by my side along the way.

Kevin...for your true will and determination in helping me set myself free.

Jim...for making me believe I am a writer and for your sweet guidance to dig deeper and bring this book alive.

Clint...for fulfilling my dream of becoming your wife and the mother I always dreamed of being to our amazing girls.

ABOUT THE AUTHOR

KORI CLAUSEN has never considered herself a writer. She still doesn't. While she has accomplished a series of amazing things in her life, including an international dance career, running a restaurant, working as a renowned yoga instructor, organizing charity events and raising her four amazing daughters, she never thought "author" would be on that list. She blames her husband Clint, who passed a few years ago. In fact, she's more than a little convinced that Clint is actually the one writing this book and she's just serving as his vessel. And she's OK with that; he always enjoyed the limelight a little more than she did. Just as with the years she got to spend married to him, she's simply happy to be a part of the journey.

JIM MARTYKA is an award-winning freelance journalist and writer living in Los Angeles. He has worked on over twenty published works (and many more in production) as an author, co-author, ghostwriter and/or editor, including the very successful autobiography of Hall of Fame football player Willie Davis called *Closing the Gap* and the best-selling *The Eight Characters of Comedy* by renowned acting coach Scott Sedita. He is also the co-founder of the L.A.-based theatre company Theatre Unleashed and the production company Hold For Plane Pictures, as well as an actor, musician, playwright and screenwriter.

A VOLLEYBALL TOURNAMENT IN HONOR OF
CLINT AND TO PROMOTE
PREVENTIVE HEART SCREENINGS
4dfours.com

SCHEDULE A HEART SCREENING HERE
providence.org/locations/plcm-torrance/cardiovascular-center-of-excellence/heart-screening

KORI'S STORY FROM MOONDTIDE MEDIA
moontidemedia.com/four-daughters

KORI'S WEBSITE
koriclausen.com

Made in the USA
Columbia, SC
28 January 2021